JUSTIN ANDERSON

Kibble Contracts: How To Become A Pet Influencer

"I think having an animal in your life makes you a better human."

– Rachel Ray

Contents

1

Introduction to the Paw-some World of Pet Influencers

Understanding the Rise of Pet Influencers

Pet influencers have taken social media by storm in recent years. Cute and cuddly cats, dogs, and even the occasional exotic animal have captured the hearts and feeds of millions of followers. But where did this phenomenon come from, and what's driving its explosive growth? This section dives into the emergence of pet influencers, their impact, and the key factors fueling their popularity.

The Emergence of Pet Influencers

The concept of pets developing their own media presence traces back over a century to early Hollywood animal stars like Rin Tin Tin. But the age of pet influencers really began in the early 2010s with cats like **Grumpy Cat** gaining viral fame. Since then, the petfluencer world has grown exponentially.

Early Examples of Pet Influencers

- Grumpy Cat: With her perpetually grumpy expression, this feline became one of the first major pet influencers. She amassed millions of followers across social media in the early 2010s.
- Boo the Pomeranian: Dubbed the "World's Cutest Dog," Boo became a sensation on Facebook with over 16 million followers. He published a book and even had his own merch line.
- Marnie the Dog: Adopted at age 11, this senior rescue dog charmed fans with her tongue-out smile. She garnered over 2 million Instagram followers before passing away in 2019.

Key Moments in the Rise of Pet Influencing

- 2012 – The first wave of viral pet fame with Grumpy Cat. This sparked interest in pets developing their own media brands.
- 2014 – Instagram takes off. Pet owners start creating accounts for their photogenic companions.
- 2015 – Pets land major brand deals. Grumpy Cat stars in a Friskies cat food campaign.
- 2017 – Pet influencer marketing emerges. Brands begin leveraging pet influencers for sponsored content.
- 2022 – Pet influencers turn into big business. Some reportedly earn over $50k for a single sponsored post.

Understanding the Appeal of Pet Content
What makes pet content so irresistible to millions of people?

Studies highlight a few psychological factors:

- It triggers the release of *oxytocin*, the "feel good" hormone associated with emotional bonds.
- Their antics tap into our innate sense of playfulness.
- It provides a respite from negativity online. Pet pics offer a morale boost.

Analyzing the Impact of Pet Influencers

Pet influencers may seem frivolous on the surface, but they've had surprising impacts across pop culture, consumer trends, and society.

Influence on Pet Product Trends

Pet brands pay big bucks for sponsorships to capitalize on their sway. Some notable examples:

- A certain car hammock went viral after Marutaro the Shiba Inu laid across one. Sales spiked.
- Catnip toys inspired by famous felines consistently top Amazon rankings.
- Even pet food brands try to align themselves with influencer pets.

Shifting Perceptions of Pets in Society

Pet influencers have helped transform how we view and treat companion animals:

- More pets are now seen as family members vs. property. Influencers portray their close bonds.
- It's become trendy to lavish pets with over-the-top toys

and accessories.
- Pets gain more autonomy and agency through their own social media accounts.

Case Studies: Pets That Changed the Game
Certain pet pioneers paved the way for current influencers:

- Lil Bub: One of the first pets to sign major endorsement deals and star in TV specials. She raised over $700k for charity too.
- Doug the Pug: With over 18 million followers, his popularity kicked off the pug influencer craze.
- Jiffpom: As the first pet to get 10 million+ followers, he set records and raised awareness.

Factors Behind Their Popularity

Pet influencers have clearly tapped into something special. What explains why followers can't get enough cat and dog content?

The Emotional Connection with Animals

People form real attachments and relationships with pets they've never met. It taps into our instinctive love of animals.

The Role of Visual Content in Pet Influencing

The visual nature of platforms like Instagram suits cute, eye-catching pet pics perfectly. It's all about capturing their charm.

Social Media Algorithms and Pet Content

Algorithms favor pet content. Pet influencer posts tend to get higher engagement, so platforms boost their reach.

Crafting a Unique Pet Influencer Identity

Starting a successful pet influencer profile requires thoughtful branding and identity creation. Here's how to develop an authentic online persona that attracts a loyal following.

Defining Your Pet's Brand

Pinpoint what makes your pet special to shape their brand story:

Identifying Your Pet's Unique Traits

- Look beyond basic facts like breed, age, and name. Dig into their personality.
- What quirks or behaviors capture their charm? Do they have any signature moves?
- What is their backstory? Adoption details often resonate.

Aligning Your Pet's Brand with Your Audience

- Appeal to specific demographics. New parents may especially love a pet who adores kids.
- Consider niche interests like travel or fitness to attract enthusiasts.
- Spotlight causes that matter to amplify your pet's impact.

Creating a Brand Story for Your Pet

- Outline your pet's origin story, interests, quirks, causes, and dreams!
- Integrate your pet's perspective to build an emotional

connection with the audience.

Building a Distinctive Online Persona

Strategically craft content that brings out your pet's unique charm:

Developing a Consistent Voice and Style

- Maintain the same first-person perspective and speaking style.
- Infuse your pet's personality into captions. Are they sassy? Sophisticated? Sweet?
- Reply to comments in a way that fits their persona.

Visual Branding: Imagery and Aesthetics

- Curate a cohesive theme with colors and editing style.
- Use props or backdrops that complement your pet's image.
- Take photos capturing your pet's best angles and expressions.

Engaging Your Audience with Your Pet's Persona

- Give followers a window into your pet's daily adventures to build a connection.
- Share funny mishaps that followers can relate to.
- Celebrate exciting milestones like birthdays or Gotcha Days.

Strategies for Authenticity

Authenticity is crucial for pet influencers to foster genuine engagement:
Balancing Personal and Promotional Content

- Mix in plenty of everyday moments along with sponsorships. Followers want to see real life!
- Even for sponsorships, focus on creating authentic experiences with the product.

Keeping It Real: Avoiding Over-Curation

- It's OK if photos aren't perfectly composed or your pet misbehaves! Relatable flaws can charm followers.
- Post fresh, candid moments rather than overly editing content.

Engaging with Followers Genuinely

- Maintain personal interactions by liking and responding to comments.
- Share user-generated content and thank creators. This builds community.

Establishing Your Pet on Social Media Platforms

Choosing the right platforms and optimizing your content strategy can take your pet influencer profile to the next level.

Choosing the Right Platforms

Assess each site based on your goals, audience, and content plans:

Evaluating Different Social Media Platforms

- Instagram: Ideal for visual content and "day in the life" storytelling. Very pet friendly.
- Facebook: Allows deeper connections with fans in Groups. Strong for community.
- TikTok: Shares short videos that can capture funny pet moments. Has huge reach.
- YouTube: Good platform for training, advice, longer videos. Monetizable.

Tailoring Your Approach to Each Platform

- Play to the strengths of each platform's format. More visual on Instagram, conversational on Facebook.
- Optimize content for each site. Short-form videos for TikTok, tutorials for YouTube.

Pros and Cons of Major Social Media Sites for Pet Influencers

- Instagram: Highly visual and engaging but lots of competition. Limited monetization.
- Facebook: Builds loyal communities but group engagement takes time.
- YouTube: Monetization opportunities but requires high-quality long-form video.
- TikTok: Trendy platform with huge growth, but content

can get lost quickly. Viral potential.

Creating Engaging Content

Post content designed to delight pet lovers:
Types of Content That Resonate with Pet Lovers

- Cute moments: snuggling, playtime, sleepy pets
- Humorous antics: burrito'ed in blankets, startled reactions
- Relatable experiences: vet visits, new toys/treats, travel woes

Planning and Scheduling Content

- Maintain a consistent posting schedule, like daily or a few times per week.
- Use social media scheduling tools to plan content in advance when possible.

Using Stories, Reels, and Live Sessions Effectively

- Share quick snapshots in the moment on Stories.
- Edit playful or silly footage into short Reels.
- Go Live showcasing your pet's daily adventures.

Growing Your Pet's Social Media Presence

Expand your pet's audience consistently over time with smart tactics:
Organic Growth Strategies

- Utilize relevant hashtags, especially niche pet tags.
- Engage with your audience by liking and commenting.
- Cross-promote content across your other social profiles.

Collaborating with Other Pet Influencers

- Coordinate giveaways or contests together.
- Share each other's content and engage with it.
- Guest post pet influencer features or videos.

Leveraging Trends and Seasonal Content

- Ride viral pet moments like #dogsoftiktok trends.
- Post holiday costumes or photos for seasonal engagement.

The world of pet influencers offers endless possibilities to creatively engage audiences. As more pets build their personal brands, the opportunities continue growing. But with the right strategic foundation focusing on quality connections over quantity, your pet can carve out their own space in this dynamic niche.

2

Crafting Your Pet's Online Persona

Developing a compelling online persona is key for pet influencers to capture attention and build an audience. This chapter explores strategies for accentuating your pet's unique identity across platforms through authenticity and engaging storytelling.

Developing a Unique Identity for Your Pet

Your pet's natural charm and quirks are the foundation for their distinctive brand. Bring out their personality online.

Finding Your Pet's Unique Characteristics

Get to know your pet on a deeper level to unearth their special traits.

Identifying Personality Traits and Quirks

- What are your pet's defining attributes? Playful? Regal? Goofy?

- Spotlight endearing behaviors like funny sleeping positions or play routines.
- Use questionnaires to assess your pet's **personality type**.

Embracing Your Pet's Natural Behavior

- Capture candid moments that highlight your pet's authentic self.
- Let your pet's interests guide content themes, like beach trips for water loving dogs.
- Don't try to force them into roles that don't suit their true nature.

Storytelling Through Your Pet's Unique Features

- Develop origin stories based on unique traits like unusual markings.
- Create adventures around your pet's favorite activities.
- Turn quirky behaviors into recurring comedic themes.

Creating a Consistent Online Persona

Strategically develop your pet's brand identity across platforms.

Aligning Visual Style with Personality

- Maintain consistent editing, filters, and imagery styles that complement your pet's persona.
- Incorporate props or backdrops that accentuate their distinctive traits.

Consistency Across Different Platforms

- Adapt content style to each platform while retaining the same core identity.
- Use unified profile photos, bios, and handles to maintain cohesion across sites.

Building a Recognizable Brand for Your Pet

- Establish branding assets like custom graphics, logos, or merchandise.
- Curate a hashtag library with branded tags fans can use.
- Cultivate a defined niche and perspective that sets your pet apart.

Showcasing Your Pet's Personality

Let your pet's authentic self shine through engaging content approaches.

Engaging Content That Reflects Your Pet's Identity

- Develop recurring segments or types of posts tailored to your pet's interests.
- Infuse their unique perspective and voice into photo captions and video narration.

Mixing Humor and Authenticity

- Leverage your pet's silly antics for laugh-out-loud moments.
- Balance humorous content with raw, candid slices of real

life.

Case Studies of Successful Pet Personas

- Esther the Wonder Pig: Built a brand around her playful, positive personality.
- Dogumentary: Showcases the adventurous spirit of Shiba Inu Sam through travel docs.
- Harlow the Weimaraner: Her modeling photoshoots play up her elegant, larger-than-life diva persona.

Accentuating Your Pet's Charm and Quirks

Thoughtful content strategies can highlight what makes your pet magnetically endearing.

Highlighting Unique Traits

Get creative with how you present your pet's distinctive attributes.

Emphasizing Distinctive Physical Attributes

- Zoom in on unusual markings, expressions, or features.
- Take photos from angles that flatter their physique or faces.
- Dress up your pet to complement natural assets like beautiful fur.

Showcasing Rare or Unique Behaviors

- Document one-of-a-kind talents like painting, skate-

boarding, or dancing.
- Film behaviors rarely captured like barking, howling, or zoomies.
- Turn quirky habits into recurring content segments.

Creative Ways to Feature Your Pet's Best Qualities

- Photo series: Capture your pet's silly sleep positions.
- Montages: Combine clips showing your pet's range of expressions.
- Polls: Ask fans which of your pet's features they find cutest.

Building a Narrative Around Your Pet

Develop engaging themes and stories starring your pet.
Creating Engaging Stories and Themes

- Craft themed adventures like a sailing excursion for a water-loving dog.
- Document a day-in-the-life following your pet's daily routine.
- Imagine stories from your pet's perspective using their voice.

Using Your Pet's Quirks to Tell a Story

- Turn funny habits into character traits, like an "addiction" to bully sticks.
- Personify behaviors by imagining their motivation, like your cat "helping" with yoga.

- Let your pet's interests drive recurring content themes.

Developing a Content Calendar Around Your Pet's Life

- Plan posts highlighting upcoming milestones like birthdays.
- Build anticipation for events like vet visits or vacations.
- Spread awareness for causes important to your pet, like shelter volunteering.

Engaging with Your Audience

Foster meaningful connections by bringing fans into your pet's world.

Interacting with Followers Through Your Pet's Persona

- Respond to comments using your pet's voice as if they're speaking directly to fans.
- Ask followers questions to spur conversation from your pet's perspective.

Encouraging Audience Participation

- Crowdsource content ideas from followers tailored to your pet's interests and personality.
- Share user-generated content related to your pet, like fan art.

Building a Community Around Your Pet's Character

- Develop hashtags, merchandise, or hang-out events to

unite your pet's fans.
- Facilitate discussions and forums for followers to connect over their shared appreciation of your pet.

Captivating an Audience with Authenticity

Genuine interactions are crucial for establishing trust and loyalty with followers.

The Importance of Authenticity in Pet Influencing

Staying true to your pet fosters more meaningful connections. Staying True to Your Pet's Nature

- Avoid forcing your pet into unnatural scenarios just for content.
- Let your pet take the lead in determining content themes and activities.
- Be willing to showcase real challenges alongside curated moments.

The Impact of Authenticity on Audience Engagement

- Authenticity builds trust and rapport with followers.
- Relatable imperfections and challenges humanize your pet.
- Transparency helps followers feel invested in your pet's story.

Avoiding the Pitfalls of Over-Staging

17

- Overly performative content can look disingenuous.
- Recreating viral behaviors repeatedly dilutes the moment's authenticity.
- Followers crave candid moments that reveal your pet's true self.

Balancing Online Presence and Your Pet's Well-being

Prioritize your pet's comfort over producing content.
Ensuring Your Pet's Comfort and Safety

- Only feature your pet in ways they naturally enjoy. Never force it.
- Monitor for signs of stress and cease activities that provoke anxiety.
- Set boundaries around appropriate handling and interaction.

Recognizing Signs of Stress or Discomfort

- Warning signs include cowering, aggression, excessive panting or shedding.
- Pay attention to subtle body language like ear position, pupil dilation, and lip-licking.
- If in doubt, assume your pet needs a break. Their well-being comes first.

Maintaining a Healthy Balance Between Online and Offline Life

- Avoid overexposing your pet or obsessively documenting

every moment.
- Preserve special offline experiences just for your pet away from social media.
- Take regular digital detoxes to reconnect and recharge.

Building a Loyal and Engaged Following

Authenticity fosters powerful connections with your supporters.

Fostering Genuine Connections with Followers

- Show appreciation for thoughtful comments with genuine, individualized responses.
- Share personal challenges to form mutual understanding and support.

Sharing Real-Life Experiences and Challenges

- Let fans into behind-the-scenes moments, not just highlight reels.
- Discuss real issues transparently like health problems or losses.

Creating a Sense of Community Among Followers

- Facilitate discussions enabling followers to connect.
- Spotlight fan tributes and foster a culture of mutual support.
- Organize meet-ups for fans bonding over shared love for your pet.

Showcasing your pet's authentic charm and building a real connection with supporters is key for influencer longevity. By embracing your pet's quirks and crafting engaging narratives, your pet can truly establish their one-of-a-kind online identity.

3

Finding Your Furry Friend's Niche

Selecting a specific niche for your pet provides direction and helps attract ideal followers. This chapter covers evaluating niches based on your pet's talents, planning niche content strategies, and positioning your pet as an authority.

Identifying the Right Niche for Your Pet

Start by assessing your pet's natural abilities and preferences.

Assessing Your Pet's Interests and Skills

Get to know your pet's innate qualities to pick a fulfilling niche.

Observing Your Pet's Natural Inclinations

- Take note of activities they gravitate towards and enjoy.
- Pay attention to behaviors that come naturally to them.
- Identify talents like athleticism, intelligence, or friendliness.

Aligning Your Pet's Interests with Potential Niches

- Active, energetic pets may thrive in sports/adventure.
- Fashionable pets can rock couture in a style niche.
- Pets with artist talent can create in a creative niche.

Evaluating Your Pet's Suitability for Different Niches
Consider their...

- Temperament: Avoid niches with excessive handling for anxious pets.
- Physical abilities: Factor in age, mobility, and health.
- Training: Some niches like entertainment require specialized skills.

Researching Market Trends and Niches

Analyze the current pet influencer landscape for underserved niches.
Analyzing Current Trends in Pet Influencing

- Use tools like **Buzzsumo** to identify top-performing pet niches.
- Study rapid growth hashtags indicating emerging trends. #Reelsdog and #Adventuredog are rising fast.

Identifying Gaps in the Pet Influencer Market

- Look for niches with few established influencers like reptile/exotics.
- Combine multiple niches like senior pet fitness.

- Local pet travel content for specific regions can fill a need.

Leveraging Your Pet's Uniqueness in a Specific Niche

- Showcase one-of-a-kind talents like surfing, art, or dancing.
- Feature unique attributes like distinct markings or rare breeds.
- Share niche experiences as the only pet influencer in space.

Finalizing Your Niche Choice

Select a niche that sets your pet up for long-term success.
Considering Long-Term Viability

- Will niche appeal remain consistent over time?
- Does the niche offer enough content variety?

Balancing Market Demand with Your Pet's Comfort

- Avoid oversaturated niches like cute puppies.
- Don't force your pet into an unsuitable niche just for attention.

Establishing a Clear Niche Focus

- Having a defined niche helps attract ideal followers.
- You can gradually expand your niche over time once established.

Strategizing for Niche-Specific Content

Create tailored content that engages your niche audience.

Planning Content Around Your Niche

Map out content that spotlights your niche.
Developing a Content Strategy Aligned with Your Niche

- Create content formats that showcase your niche like underwater photos for aquatic pets.
- Plan recurring content segments like Therapy Dog Monday.
- Feature niche-specific topics like reviews of adventure gear for outdoor pets.

Creating a Content Mix (Educational, Entertainment, Inspirational)

- Educate with care tutorials for grooming niches.
- Entertain with funny niche mishaps like sports bloopers.
- Inspire with senior pet fitness motivational quotes.

Scheduling and Seasonal Considerations for Niche Content

- Align content with seasonal niche hooks like holiday costumes.
- Time evergreen niche content like food roundups for maximum exposure.

Engaging with Niche Audiences

Tailor your messaging and outreach to your niche fans.
Tailoring Your Message to Appeal to Niche Audiences

- Use niche-specific terminology and hashtags followers will recognize.
- Emphasize how your niche content solves problems or meets needs for that group.

Leveraging Niche-Specific Hashtags and Trends

- Research relevant hashtags to incorporate like #AdventureDog for outdoor pets.
- Monitor niche hashtag trends you can tap into at the right moment.

Collaborating with Influencers and Brands Within Your Niche

- Guest post to share your niche perspective with overlap audiences.
- Partner with complementary niche brands on sponsorships or giveaways.

Measuring and Adapting Your Strategy

Continuously refine your approach based on data and insights.
Analyzing Engagement and Feedback

- Track niche content performance with metrics like saves

25

and comments.

- Solicit follower feedback on niche content ideas.

Refining Your Approach Based on Insights

- Double down on top-performing niche content formats.
- Try new niche content styles that followers request.

Staying Flexible and Responsive to Change in Your Niche

- Watch for declining interest signals like falling engagement.
- Be ready to shift gears if your niche declines or saturates.

Positioning Your Pet for Maximum Impact

Strategically establish your authority and expand your reach within your niche.

Establishing a Strong Position in Your Niche

Stand out with signature content and brand assets.
Building a Brand that Stands Out in Your Niche

- Create original branded hashtag campaigns followers can participate in.
- Design custom niche-themed graphics and merchandise.
- Claim niche-defining social handles like @Adventure-Dogs.

Creating Signature Content or Campaigns

- Produce recurring niche content exclusively associated with your pet like a travel series.
- Launch large-scale campaigns like a niche photo contest.

Establishing Credibility and Expertise in Your Niche

- Demonstrate extensive niche knowledge in educational content.
- Feature "behind-the-scenes" insights from niche experiences.
- Interview established niche experts or brands.

Leveraging Social Media Algorithms

Learn to play the algorithm game to maximize niche content reach.

Understanding Algorithm Dynamics for Better Reach

- Study how niche posting times and formats influence reach.
- Analyze competitors' top-performing content strategies.

Optimizing Content for Maximum Visibility

- Use high-performing niche hashtags and strategic captions.
- Produce engaging niche video and photo content algorithms favor.

Staying Updated with Platform Changes and Trends

- Follow niche influencer community discussions around algorithm updates.
- Continuously test new platform features and content formats.

Expanding Beyond Your Niche

Gradually introduce more diverse content without diluting your core niche.

Exploring Opportunities for Cross-Niche Collaboration

- Partner with complementary niches like fashion x grooming.
- Participate in broader hashtag trends like #DogsofTikTok that align.

Gradually Introducing Diverse Content

- Test different content verticals and analyze performance.
- Over time, increase ratio of general content as your audience broadens.

Balancing Niche Focus with Broader Appeal

- Feature niche-focused series alongside universally appealing content like cute posts.
- Maintain your niche as the core of your content strategy.

Defining a niche creates a content road map to follow while allowing flexibility to evolve over time. Position your pet strategically at the forefront of your niche to make a lasting impact.

4

Beyond the Trends: Maintaining Authenticity as a Pet Influencer

In the fast-paced world of social media, pet influencers are constantly bombarded with new trends. From viral challenges to popular audios, it's tempting to jump on every trend in hopes of increased engagement. However, blindly chasing trends can compromise your pet's unique brand identity. The key is to thoughtfully adopt trends that align with your pet's personality while preserving authenticity.

Navigating Social Media Trends Strategically

Social media trends come and go swiftly. As a pet influencer, it's crucial to identify and participate in relevant trends judiciously.

Pinpoint Trends Relevant to Your Niche

Rather than reacting to every trend, be selective. Regularly research popular hashtags and trending topics related specifically to pets and animals. Analyze engagement on trending posts from influencers in your niche. This allows you to filter out irrelevant trends.

Evaluate Trend Alignment with Your Brand Personality

Before participating, determine if the trend resonates with your pet's brand identity and voice. A trend centered around showing off athletic abilities may not suit a senior arthritic cat. Carefully consider whether the trend complements or contradicts your brand.

Balance Trend Participation with Brand Authenticity

Avoid over-reliance on trends at the expense of authenticity. Participate in select trends that organically align with your brand personality, rather than force-fitting trend participation. Trends should complement, not define, your content.

Adapt Trends Creatively to Your Brand

Rather than participating in trends verbatim, adapt them to reflect your pet's unique brand.

Customize Trends to Your Brand Voice

Add your own spin by recreating trends using your pet's distinctive persona. Infuse the captions, audio, props, settings, and visuals with your brand's tone and style.

Participate in Trends Authentically

Trends shouldn't feel forced. Capture your pet genuinely engaging with trends aligned to their interests. For example, an energetic dog may naturally enjoy participating in active dance challenges.

Examine Trend Examples Done Right

Study influencers who participate in trends while staying true to their brand identities. Analyze how they adapt trends to resonate with their audience rather than blindly replicating them.

Avoid the Pitfalls of Trend-Chasing

Indiscriminate trend-chasing often becomes a race to the bottom. Be mindful of these risks:

Recognize When a Trend Doesn't Fit Your Brand

No matter how viral, avoid trends that require your pet to stray far from their brand identity. For example, an anxious pet may be stressed by disruptive challenges.

Beware Relying Too Heavily on Trends

While timely use of trends can attract new followers, over-dependence on trending topics often leads to a decline in originality and authenticity. Find a healthy balance.

Maintain Brand Integrity Amidst Fads

Viral trends come and go, but your brand identity should remain constant. Withstand the pressure to conform by staying committed to creating content that genuinely resonates with your audience.

Keep Your Pet's Unique Identity at the Forefront

While participating in select trends, always keep your pet's authentic self as the focal point.

Define Your Pet's Distinctive Qualities and Character

Go beyond basic descriptors like breed and age. Dig deeper into small quirks, subtle mannerisms, and endearing habits that reveal your pet's identity. Keep these top of mind.

Ensure Content Consistently Reflects Your Pet's True Self

Let your pet's genuine personality and interest shine through in all posts. For example, create toy review videos catered to their favorite playstyle - chasing, fetching, destroying.

Authenticity Builds Lasting Engagement

Followers deeply connect with seeing your pet's real self. Flaunting wealth or popularity temporarily boosts vanity metrics but erodes audience loyalty. Authenticity fosters true engagement.

Balance Business Success with Authenticity

Monetizing your influence must not come at the cost of your pet's wellbeing and brand identity.

Ensure Paid Partnerships Align with Your Pet's Brand Values

Select collaborations mindfully to avoid compromising your brand for money. Decline promotions for products your pet wouldn't genuinely use or that lack transparency.

Limit Commercialization

Avoid over-commercializing your pet's image through relentless merchandise plugs, intrusive ads, and sponsored content that eclipses their authentic personality.

Prioritize Your Pet's Comfort and Joy

Never force your pet into content for financial gain. Monitor for signs of stress. Your pet's happiness trumps monetization metrics and analytics.

Maintain a Clear, Consistent Brand Message

Cement your pet's brand identity through consistent messaging that resonates with your audience.

Develop a Succinct Brand Message That Encapsulates Your Pet

Summarize your pet influencer brand into a short tagline or statement that captures their essence.

Reinforce Your Message Across All Platforms and Content

Integrate your brand statement into profiles, headers, captions, posts, and partnerships. Repetition cements retention.

Periodically Re-evaluate and Refine Your Brand Messaging

As your pet's brand evolves, reassess if your messaging still accurately reflects the brand identity. Make subtle changes as needed.

Adopt Trends Selectively After Rigorous Vetting

Participate in trends sparingly and only after careful consideration.

Establish Criteria for Trend Approval

Develop guidelines, including relevance to your brand voice, appeal to your target audience, and long-term brand implications.

Plan Trend Adoption into Your Content Strategy

Map out a quarterly content calendar, balancing evergreen content that displays your pet's authentic self with limited trend participation.

Analyze Performance of Trend Content

Use metrics like reach and engagement rate to compare trend content against evergreen content. Assess what resonates most with your audience.

Learn From Trends to Improve Your Brand

Observe how top pet influencers adapt trends while remaining authentic. Let trends point out new content formats, features, and strategies to enhance your brand.

The allure of viral trends can be intense but pet influencers must refrain from blind bandwagon-jumping. By staying laser focused on your pet's authentic identity and selectively adopting only relevant trends, you can achieve an optimal balance between capitalizing on temporary virality and building an enduring brand.

5

Engagement Over Numbers: Building Meaningful Connections as a Pet Influencer

In the influencer sphere, follower count is often touted as the holy grail of social media success. However, for pet influencers looking to build an enduring brand and monetize effectively, the quality of engagement you foster matters far more than vanity metrics. Let's explore why engagement should be your true north, and how to leverage it for brand partnerships and income.

Why Engagement Matters More Than Followers

A substantial follower count may seem impressive, but without authentic engagement, it holds little value. Here's why quality connections matter more:

Followers Can Be Purchased or Inorganic

Follower counts are easy to artificially inflate through paid services, follow/unfollow techniques, and bots. But bought followers are worthless for branding.

Vanity Metrics Don't Equal Influence

Followers may subscribe for cute pet photos without truly engaging with or promoting your brand. Your influence stems from those passionately interacting with your content.

Engagement Fuels Brand Discovery

Consistent engagement increases your brand's visibility and reach organically. When followers actively like, comment, and share your posts, the algorithm amplifies your content.

It Cultivates a Loyal Community

Rich engagement denotes followers who deeply connect with your pet and brand. This community is more likely to passionately support you long-term and serve as brand advocates.

How to Measure Meaningful Engagement

Focus on these key metrics to assess engagement quality:

Post Interactions

Analyze likes, comments, shares, saves, follows, DMs, clicks, and other post interactions. Are people thoughtfully interacting or just scrolling?

Account Mentions and Tags

Track brand mentions and tags outside your account as it shows your community organically talks about your brand.

Audience Retention

Notice follower fluctuations. Growing retention signals you captivate your audience. Declining retention indicates disengagement.

Conversion Rates

Monitor what percentage of followers purchase products or donate to causes you promote. High conversion equals influence.

Ways to Foster Meaningful Engagement

It takes effort to cultivate genuine bonds with followers. Apply these tactics:

Show Your Pet's Authentic Self

Followers deeply connect with seeing your pet's unfiltered personality, quirks, and adventures. Authenticity builds emotional investment.

Engage Beyond Your Content

Reply to comments, hold live talks, and interact beyond just posting content. Being accessible helps strengthen ties.

Reward Loyal Followers

Spotlight long-term supporters through bonuses like special discounts, exclusive content access, and brand ambassadorships.

Encourage Two-Way Interactions

Solicit follower opinions through polls and questions. This makes them feel valued as part of your community.

Leveraging Engagement for Brand Partnerships

For pet influencers, quality engagement truly matters when securing lucrative brand collaborations.

Prove Your Influence to Brands

Brands want confidence you can drive real awareness and sales. Robust engagement metrics substantiate your influence.

Command Higher Rates

Pet influencers with higher engagement can justify larger partnership fees since their community is invested. Vanity followers don't warrant high rates.

Attract Relevant Brand Partners

Deep engagement demonstrates your niche community and the types of brands you can authentically promote to them.

Build Trust for Recommendations

When followers are engaged, they trust your assessments of products or services. This trust enables natural recommendations.

Monetizing Through Engaged Followers

Loyal followers are key to generating income. Here's how to profit from quality engagement:

Direct Purchases and Donations

Highly engaged followers are happy to support you financially through buying merchandise, gifts, or donating to causes.

Affiliate Programs and Links

Engaged followers are more likely to purchase products you recommend through affiliated links, earning you commission.

Premium Content and Memberships

Superfans will readily pay for exclusive digital content and insider access through premium memberships.

Influencer Events and Meetups

Devoted local followers may attend ticketed live events like pet influencer meet and greets.

   While rapid follower growth is tempting, stay laser focused on building authentic engagement and community. Valuing quality over quantity will pay dividends for your personal brand and income. Let your pet's #realinfluence speak for itself.

Fostering Engagement Through Social Listening

Listening to your audience provides priceless insights into their interests and values. Here are ways to tune in:

Monitoring Mentions and Hashtags

Stay on pulse of what followers are saying about your pet by tracking relevant tags and keywords. This reveals current buzz and sentiment.

Analyzing Comment Trends

Notice which posts prompt the most dialogue. This indicates your audience's priorities. Leaning into these conversations deepens engagement.

Polling Followers

Survey your audience directly through polls asking what content they want to see more of. This guides your strategy.

Reading DMs and Reviews

Both public and private direct feedback further highlight what resonates most with your community. Incorporate this input.

Tracking Competitors

See what content other pet influencers create that generates high engagement. Apply those learnings to your own brand.

Optimizing Content Categories for Engagement

Tailor content to your followers' preferences for maximum response.

Play to Your Pet's Strengths

Showcase your pet doing what they enjoy most, whether it's learning tricks, unboxing toys, or relaxing. Followers connect with authenticity.

Align Content with Audience Interests

If your followers respond most to traveling content, create more road trip and pet friendly destination posts.

Experiment with Emerging Formats

Test viral formats like stories, reels, and livestreams. Track engagement growth potential.

Localize Content

Produce posts showcasing your hometown or city. Local followers appreciate seeing familiar spots.

Balance Education and Entertainment

Combine fun posts with informational content like pet care, training, and product reviews. This appeals to all followers.

Avoiding Tactics that Inflate Vanity Metrics

Beware measures that artificially increase followers without engagement:

Buying Followers or Likes

It's tempting to pay for followers but it damages your brand authenticity when engagement doesn't align.

Follow/Unfollow

This blackhat tactic artificially pumps followers but tanks engagement rate, raising red flags.

Overusing Hashtags

Hashtag stuffing only drives empty followers. Use relevant hashtags selectively for targeted reach.

Over-posting

Posting too frequently pushes your content to the bottom of feeds, reducing visibility and engagement.

Paying for Visibility

Avoid services promoting posts or accounts. Focus on content and community for organic growth.

Remember, social media is about people, not numbers. By forging authentic connections with your audience, your pet can build an influencer brand that stands the test of time. Valueless vanity metrics can never replace true engagement.

Engagement-Building Content Ideas

Brainstorm fresh ideas that encourage audience interactivity:

- Pet costume try-on hauls
- DIY pet toy tutorials
- Pet-themed trivia or giveaways
- Meet the sibling/friend posts
- Pet opinion polls
- Pet care or training Q&As
- Unboxing monthly pet boxes
- Pet decor DIY projects
- Pet gift guides and reviews
- Pet-friendly travel guides
- Day in the life vlogs
- Fan highlight features
- Pet meetup announcements
- Collaborations with fellow pet influencers
- Pet holiday celebration posts
- Pet-centric meme roundups
- Behind-the-scenes creator vlogs

Get creative with formats like stories, reels, and lives that lend themselves to engaging dialogues. Avoid set-it-and-forget-it content that discourages connections. Treat followers like friends, and your pet will flourish.

Executing Giveaways and Contests Ethically

Giveaways can engage followers but often devolve into like-grabbing tactics. Here are best practices:

- Clearly outline giveaway rules, entry criteria, timeframe, and selection process upfront. No loopholes or surprises.
- Keep entry requirements simple like follows, tags, shares, or comments. Avoid excessive hoop-jumping.
- Manually select winners fairly at random versus shady apps. Be transparent by showing the selection.
- Limit entries to one per person. Block giveaway accounts to prevent inflated entries.
- Offer prizes that genuinely benefit followers rather than leftover inventory.
- Space out giveaways. Too many comes off as manipulative.
- Follow FTC giveaway guidelines like clear sponsor disclosure and eligibility limitations.

The key is ensuring giveaways are designed to thank and engage your community rather than simply drive follower metrics. Authenticity and transparency will serve you well.

Pitfalls of Pay-for-Play Collaborations

When partnering with brands, prioritize alignment over money:

Avoid Obligatory Sponsorships

Turn down sponsorships with brands you wouldn't authentically recommend or that don't resonate with your audience. Follower trust is hard-earned and easily lost.

Be Wary of Mismatched Products

Avoid prematurely pushing your pet into human-focused collaborations like makeup or fashion solely for money. It reeks of inauthenticity.

Don't Let Money Dictate Content

Refuse content creation requests that betray your pet's comfort and identity like dangerous stunts or extensive travel. Your pet always comes first.

Read Contracts Thoroughly

Scrutinize contracts to ensure reasonable expectations, fair pay, and brand transparency around usage rights and obligations.

Limit Promotional Content

Balance occasional sponsorships with diverse organic content. Overt advertising repels engaged followers in favor of sales targets.

Stay true to your pet's brand identity. Profitable partnerships will organically follow authentic connections.

6

Strategies to Boost Your Pet's Online Presence

Having an online presence for your pet can be an incredibly fun and rewarding way to connect with other pet lovers. Whether you're looking to make your furry friend Instagram famous or simply want to share cute photos with friends and family, growing and engaging an online audience takes strategy and consistency. In this chapter, we'll explore proven tactics to enhance your pet's social media channels, collaborate with others, diversify content across platforms, and measure performance. Follow these steps to help your pet stand out from the pack and build an impactful presence across the digital landscape.

Enhancing Social Media Engagement

The foundation for boosting your pet's online presence is enhancing engagement on key social media platforms. Thoughtful content creation, maximizing hashtags and challenges, and consistent posting are critical for growth. Let's break down effective tactics in each area.

Crafting Engaging Content

Content is king when it comes to social media. Creating posts that resonate with your audience is crucial for driving engagement. Here are some tips:

Creating Content that Resonates with Your Audience

- Know your audience – Understand who is following you and what type of content they respond to most. Poll your followers to gain insights.
- Show personality – Let your pet's unique personality shine through in posts. Show their quirks through stories and captions.
- Capture candid moments – Authentic, unposed shots often connect more than staged photos.
- Leverage emotions – Posts that tap into emotions like joy, silliness and love tend to engage people.
- Tell stories – Captivate your audience by telling stories over multiple posts and videos. Build narrative and connection.

Utilizing Interactive Features (Polls, Q&As, Contests)

Take advantage of built-in interactive features on social platforms:

- Polls – Pose fun questions to your followers to get them engaged. Ex: "Which toy is Charlie's favorite?"
- Q&As – Answer common questions from followers in posts or stories. Encourage people to ask questions.

- Contests/Giveaways – Run exciting contests like photo challenges or giveaways to grow your audience.

Balancing Informative and Entertaining Posts
Strike the right balance between posts that simply entertain and those that educate:

- Humor/Cuteness – Funny memes and super cute photos tend to go viral.
- Behind-the-scenes – Give a glimpse into your daily life. Short videos work well.
- Educational – Share pet care tips, training advice, etc. Establish your expertise.
- Motivational – Uplifting quotes and affirmations attract engagement.
- Current events – Tie into holidays, events and trends when appropriate.

Maximizing Hashtags and Challenges

Strategically leveraging hashtags and social media challenges can expand your reach. Here's how:
Understanding and Using Trending Hashtags

- Research which pet hashtags are trending. (#dogs, #catsoftiktok, #petsoftiktok)
- Use a mix of popular hashtags and niche ones.
- Create branded hashtags for your pet. Ex: #CharliesAdventures

Participating in or Creating Social Media Challenges

51

- Take part in trending challenges like #posewithyourpet or create your own.
- Challenges engage followers and introduce your pet to new audiences.
- Film compilation videos of entries when launching a user-generated challenge.

Leveraging Hashtags for Greater Visibility

- Include a mix of general and specific hashtags.
- Use maximum allowed hashtags per platform without going overboard.
- Be thoughtful about which hashtags you use - choose relevant ones.

Consistent Posting and Interaction

While quality content is key, consistency and community interaction are also crucial.

Developing a Regular Posting Schedule

- Analyze your analytics to find optimal posting times.
- Post consistently in those time slots, at least 3x a week.
- Use social media planning tools to schedule posts in advance when possible.

Engaging with Followers Through Comments and Messages

- Reply to comments and questions on posts in a timely manner.
- Check direct messages daily and have conversations.

- Like and reply to comments from new followers to start relationships.

Utilizing Analytics to Optimize Posting Times

- Experiment with posting at different times and days.
- Look at when your followers are most active in analytics.
- Refine your schedule based on when engagement is highest.

Collaborations and Partnerships

Building connections with others through collaborations and partnerships can introduce your pet to new audiences.

Partnering with Other Pet Influencers

Team up on content creation with compatible pet influencers. Identifying Potential Collaboration Partners

- Look for accounts with engaged audiences and quality content.
- Seek those with similar pet personalities/interests.
- Consider following size - bigger, smaller and similar.

Coordinating Collaborative Content

- Agree on content concept and style. Align your brand identities.
- Shoot content together in person when possible.
- If not, film separately and edit together.

- Cross-promote by announcing it on both accounts.

Measuring the Success of Collaborations

- Compare engagement on collaborative posts vs your average rates.
- Did followings increase mutually after collaborating? Track growth.
- Use insights to refine tactics and find ideal partners.

Working with Brands and Sponsors

Partnering with brands through sponsorships allows monetization while growing audience reach.

Finding Brands that Align with Your Pet's Identity

- Seek brands that share similar values and personality.
- Pet care, pet fashion, pet food, and pet services are natural fits.
- Ensure the brand authentically resonates with your followers.

Establishing Successful Brand Partnerships

- Pitch professional, customized brand partnership proposals.
- Start slow, with discounted or free trial campaigns.
- Gradually increase rate as you prove your value.
- Contractually outline campaign specifics, deliverables and compensation.

Balancing Sponsored Content with Organic Posts

- Limit sponsored posts to no more than 1/3 of total content.
- Ensure sponsored content aligns stylistically with your organic content.
- Disclose #sponsored or #ad appropriately when posting partner content.

Leveraging Community and Networking

Tapping into pet influencer communities and networking can create growth opportunities.

Engaging in Pet Influencer Communities

- Join pet influencer Facebook Groups to connect.
- Attend pet influencer Meetups in your city.
- Follow, like and engage with fellow pet creators.

Networking Strategies for Building Relationships

- Comment meaningful compliments on other pet accounts.
- DM those with compatible aesthetics to start conversations.
- Offer value by making introductions, giving advice and collaborating.

Attending Industry Events for Expanded Reach

- Look for pet expos, conferences and conventions to

attend.
- Set up a booth, host a panel or sponsor events.
- Maximise in-person interactions at events for community building.

Diversifying Content Across Platforms

While focusing efforts on one or two core platforms, exploring emerging platforms and tailoring content to each can help widen your pet's audience.

Tailoring Content for Different Platforms

Each social platform has unique users and preferred content types.

Understanding the Unique Audience of Each Platform

Conduct competitor research on various platforms to identify:

- Demographic and psychographic makeup of users
- Interests, values and behavioral patterns
- What types of content resonates most

Adapting Content to Fit Platform-Specific Trends

Optimize content by platform based on your research findings:

- Instagram: polished photos, Stories, Reels, IGTV long-form vertical video
- Facebook: short videos, Stories, live video, Carousels
- YouTube: longer videos, vlogs, compilation videos

- TikTok: viral trends, challenging dances, effects, duets

Cross-Promoting Content Effectively

- Share video clips and image previews across platforms.
- Cross-post Stories.
- Link to full YouTube videos from Instagram profile.

Exploring New Platforms and Trends

Staying ahead of the curve with new platforms can help you connect with diverse audiences:
Keeping Up with Emerging Social Media Trends

- Look for buzz around new apps and features.
- Identify early adopter demographics flocking to new platforms.
- Recognize shifts in usage patterns between platforms.

Experimenting with New Platforms for Expanded Reach

- Open accounts on emerging apps with promise.
- Create platform-specific content following initial tests.
- Provide unique value to untapped audiences.

Adapting to Platform Shifts and Audience Changes

- Pivot focus and efforts if audiences migrate to new platforms.
- Fine-tune content and tone if different users respond better.

- Stay nimble and don't cling to platforms losing relevance.

Measuring and Adjusting Strategies

Analytics provide the data needed to continually refine approaches across platforms.
Using Analytics to Track Performance Across Platforms
Look at key metrics like:

- Follower growth rates
- Engagement and response rates
- Click-through rates on links
- Traffic referred from social channels

Refining Strategies Based on Engagement Data

- Double down on content styles and platforms getting traction.
- Try new tactics if current efforts aren't gaining traction.
- Review analytics weekly rather than monthly or quarterly.

Staying Agile in an Evolving Social Media Landscape

- Expect platforms to rise and fall in popularity over time.
- Consistently evaluate performance and pivot accordingly.
- Maintain a test-and-learn mindset.

Building your pet's presence online takes creativity, persistence and agility. But by implementing an integrated social strategy leveraging engaging content, strategic partnerships, multi-platform posting and performance tracking, you can unlock growth and connection. Stay nimble, leverage data, and keep your pet's personality at the forefront. With these approaches, your furry friend is sure to thrive in the digital world!

7

Monetizing Your Pet's Influence: From Engagement to Income

Turning your pet into a social media influencer takes creativity and effort. But once you've built an engaged following, how do you transform that influence into real income? This chapter explores strategies to monetize your pet's online presence through brand sponsorships, affiliate marketing, merchandise sales, premium content, events and more. Follow these tips to start earning from your furry friend's fame.

Transitioning to Monetization

Before diving headfirst into monetization, build a strong foundation and diversify revenue streams for long-term success.

Understanding the Basics of Monetization

Grasp the core concepts before developing your monetization plan.

Exploring Different Revenue Streams

Common pet influencer income sources include:

- Brand sponsorships
- Affiliate commissions
- Merchandise sales
- Paid content subscriptions
- Event tickets and sponsorships
- Expanding into other media

Balancing Monetization with Authenticity

- Avoid over-commercializing your pet's accounts.
- Vet partners thoroughly and turn down misaligned brands.
- Focus on organic content and community-building.

Setting Realistic Financial Goals

- Research typical pet influencer rates.
- Set income goals based on your follower count and engagement.
- Increase rates gradually as you prove your value.

Building a Foundation for Monetization

Establish a strong baseline of followers, engagement and brand before monetizing.

Establishing a Strong Brand and Following

- Create polished branding assets (logo, color palette, etc).
- Grow your audience through great content and community interaction.
- Make sure your pet has a clear brand identity and voice.

Creating Engaging and Shareable Content

- Produce content that resonates emotionally with viewers.
- Encourage audience participation through polls, challenges, etc.
- Develop content with viral potential.

Positioning Your Pet for Brand Deals and Sponsorships

- Highlight your expertise within your pet niche.
- Collaborate with other pet influencers.
- Pitch yourself professionally to potential sponsors.

Diversifying Income Streams

Don't rely solely on sponsorships. Explore diverse monetization avenues.

Exploring Various Monetization Avenues
Research options like:

- Affiliate marketing
- Virtual tips and classes
- Consulting or coaching services
- Online merchandise stores
- Premium content subscriptions

Balancing Direct and Indirect Monetization Methods

- Direct: Brand sponsorships, merchandise sales, events
- Indirect: Affiliate links, display ads on website

Innovating New Ways to Monetize Your Pet's Influence

- Brainstorm creative ways to generate income from your audience.
- Offer value while testing new revenue models.

Brand Partnerships and Sponsorships

For many pet influencers, brand sponsorships are the primary income source. Master this monetization channel.

Navigating Brand Deals

Landing profitable brand partnerships requires strategy and professionalism.

Identifying and Approaching Potential Sponsors

- Seek brands that align authentically with your pet's niche and style.
- Send custom partnership proposals pitching your value.

- Be persistent and follow up if you don't hear back.

Negotiating Terms and Compensation

- Start with free/discounted trial campaigns with brands.
- Gradually increase your rates as you prove ROI.
- Require detailed contracts covering compensation, deliverables and timelines.

Creating Authentic Sponsored Content

- Ensure sponsored posts match your account's style and voice.
- Disclose partnerships appropriately using #ad, #sponsored, etc.
- Limit sponsored content to no more than 30% of overall posts.

Affiliate Marketing Strategies

Earn commissions by promoting relevant products through affiliate links.

Understanding Affiliate Marketing Mechanics

- Join affiliate programs like Amazon Associates, ShareASale, etc.
- Get a unique tracking link for each product.
- Earn commission when users purchase through your link.

Selecting Relevant Affiliate Programs

- Find programs selling pet products like Chewy, PetSmart, etc.
- Ensure brands match your pet's niche and audience interests.
- Research commission rates and program reputations.

Integrating Affiliate Links Seamlessly into Content

- Discuss useful pet products naturally in posts and videos.
- Share links to featured items rather than overwhelming followers.
- Clearly disclose affiliate relationships.

Selling Merchandise and Products

Profit from branded physical and digital product sales.
Developing Pet-Influencer Branded Merchandise

- Design merchandise featuring your pet's logo and imagery.
- Ideas: T-shirts, hats, mugs, phone cases, prints.
- Use print-on-demand services like Teespring to save upfront costs.

Setting Up an Online Store

- Open a Shopify store or Etsy shop with your branded products.
- Make the shopping experience personal and on-brand.
- Optimize store for conversions with clear product photography.

Promoting and Selling Your Merchandise

- Showcase new merchandise launches on social media.
- Offer limited time sales or coupon codes to incentivize purchases.
- Send email newsletters with store promotions and launches.

Advanced Monetization Techniques

Further diversify income with paid content, events, expanding into new media and more.

Utilizing Paid Subscriptions and Exclusive Content

Engage fans through exclusive stories, videos and insights.
Exploring Platforms for Exclusive Content

- Use platforms like Patreon, Mighty Networks or Only-Fans.
- Consider launching a private Facebook group.

Developing a Strategy for Premium Content

- Identify the most in-demand type of exclusive content.
- Set subscription tiers based on demand and production efforts.
- Promote subscriptions, but don't lock all content behind a paywall.

Balancing Free and Paid Content

- Reserve premium content for subscribers, but maintain public social accounts.
- Produce a mix of free and paid content to attract new subscribers.

Hosting Events and Meet-and-Greets

Profit through ticket sales and sponsorships for online or in-person events.

Organizing Online and Offline Events

Possible events include:

- Meet-and-greet and pet photo ops
- Pet care or training webinars/classes
- Pet influencer networking mixers
- Live shows (holiday pet costume contest)

Monetizing Through Ticket Sales and Sponsorships

- Sell tickets directly or through event management platforms.
- Offer sponsorships and ambassador programs.
- Auction off special experiences or merchandise.

Leveraging Events for Brand Growth

- Share event photos and videos afterwards as content.
- Gain email subscribers by requiring sign-up to attend.
- Offer giveaways to incentivize social shares and hashtags.

Expanding into Other Media

Leverage your pet's influence into promotional opportunities beyond social media.

Exploring Opportunities in Books, TV, or Podcasts

- Pitch a book around your pet's niche or brand story.
- Look for relevant TV show interview or guest spot opportunities.
- Consider launching a pet care podcast or YouTube show.

Leveraging Your Pet's Brand in Various Media

- Repurpose social content across new media types.
- Cross-promote new media projects on social platforms.
- Use each project to expand your authority and audience.

Balancing Time Between Social Media and Other Media

- Don't spread yourself too thin across too many projects.
- Hire help for time-intensive initiatives if needed.
- Maintain consistent social posting even when expanding.

Turning pet influence into income takes thoughtfulness, creativity and persistence. By diversifying monetization strategies, providing value, and staying authentic, you can build a thriving business around your furry friend's fame. Just don't forget the fun along the way!

8

Legal and Financial Insights for Pet Influencers

Understanding Legal Aspects of Pet Influencing

Launching a pet influencing career comes with many legal considerations. As your following and income grows, it is crucial to have the proper legal protections and business structure in place. This section will explore key legal aspects of operating as a professional pet influencer.

Setting Up a Business Structure

The first major legal decision is choosing the right business entity for your pet influencer activities. There are several options to weigh:

Choosing the Right Business Entity

The most common entity types for pet influencers are sole proprietorship, partnership, LLC, and corporation. Here are some key factors to consider:

- Liability protection - LLCs and corporations provide personal liability protection that sole proprietors lack. This can be important as your business grows.
- Taxes - Sole proprietors report business income on personal returns. LLCs, partnerships and corporations allow for pass-through taxation.
- Cost and paperwork - Registering and maintaining a corporation has more administrative requirements than a sole proprietorship.
- Owner flexibility - Sole proprietorships have total control while corporations involve shareholders and corporate governance processes.

Most pet influencers opt for LLCs to get personal liability protection while retaining operational flexibility. Consult an attorney and accountant to determine the best structure for your specific situation.

Navigating Business Registration and Licensing

Properly registering your pet influencer entity is crucial for legal compliance. Key steps typically include:

- Registering your business name - File a doing business as (DBA) name if operating under anything other than your personal name.
- Forming an LLC - Creating an LLC involves filing articles of organization and paying fees.
- Obtaining licenses - Research if you need a sales tax permit or local business license based on your state and city regulations.

It is advisable to engage a business attorney to ensure you

complete all required registrations and licensing. Failing to do so can result in penalties down the line.

Understanding the Implications of Different Business Structures

Opting for an LLC or corporation does create additional legal obligations compared to a sole proprietorship. Some key responsibilities include:

- Separate finances - Business funds must be held in a separate business bank account. Personal and business finances should not intermingle.
- Meeting formalities - Corporations require shareholders meetings, appointed officers, and record keeping. LLCs also need certain formal management processes.
- Annual filings and fees - Most states require annual reports and fee payments to remain an active LLC or corporation.

Work closely with legal and accounting professionals to ensure you properly maintain your chosen business structure over time.

Intellectual Property and Brand Protection

Trademarks, copyrights, and handling infringement claims are key areas of intellectual property law for pet influencers.

Copyrights and Trademarks in Pet Influencing

As a content creator, it is crucial to understand how copyright and trademark laws apply to your work:

- Copyright - Your original photos, videos, captions, and

other creative work are automatically protected by copyright from unauthorized usage.

- Trademark - Your pet influencer name, logo, and associated brand assets can be protected through trademark registration. This prevents others from using them without permission.

Registering for copyrights and trademarks provides additional legal benefits if you ever need to enforce your intellectual property rights.

Protecting Your Content and Brand Online

Beyond formal filings, you can take proactive steps to protect your intellectual property online:

- Watermark images - Adding a watermark of your name/logo prevents unauthorized use of your photos.
- Credit all creators - If you hire others like photographers, provide proper attribution to avoid disputes over who owns the work.
- Monitor infringement - Routinely search for your name, images, and content online to find any unauthorized usage and send takedown notices.
- Register domains - Buy any domains related to your pet influencer brand so others do not cyber squat on them.

Being vigilant about policing your intellectual property helps deter theft and infringement.

Dealing with Intellectual Property Infringement

If you do discover someone using your trademarks or content without permission, typical next steps include:

- Sending a cease and desist letter - Have your attorney draft a letter demanding the infringing party stop their unauthorized usage.
- Filing a DMCA takedown - For copyright infringement online, submit a DMCA takedown request to the hosting platform.
- Pursuing legal action - For severe or unresolved cases, consider pursuing formal litigation to protect your rights and seek damages. An intellectual property attorney can advise you on the strongest avenues for recourse.

Move swiftly when infringement occurs to enforce your rights and limit damage to your brand reputation.

Navigating Contracts and Agreements

Pet influencers enter into many types of business contracts and should understand contractual fundamentals.

Understanding Contract Basics

The key elements of an enforceable contract typically include:

- Offer - One party communicates willingness to enter into a contract.
- Acceptance - The other party agrees to the contract terms.
- Consideration - Each party offers something of value. For influencers this is often content and promotion.
- Intent - Both parties agree to be bound by the contract.
- Capacity - The parties have legal ability to enter a contract.

Generally, contracts can be verbal or written. Written contracts provide stronger legal recourse if a dispute arises.

Negotiating Terms with Brands and Partners

Before signing any agreement, seek to negotiate terms that protect your interests:

- Rights - Ensure you retain rights to the content you create, including after a campaign concludes.
- Compensation - Push for fair market value compensation for your services.
- Scope - Limit usage terms so brands cannot endlessly reuse your content without limitations.
- Liabilities - Limit warranties and shift liability for issues like copyright claims to the brand.
- Termination - Include your ability to terminate for breach of contract if the brand misuses your services.

Being able to negotiate win-win terms takes confidence and experience. Know your worth and stand firm on core protections.

Seeking Legal Advice for Contractual Matters

Given the nuances of contract law, it is prudent to have an attorney review any contracts before signing, especially for high-value deals. Areas where legal expertise is particularly beneficial include:

- Reviewing fine print - Lawyers can catch restrictive clauses or conditions you might otherwise miss.
- Clarifying legal language - Attorneys explain legalese so you fully understand each provision.
- Amending terms - Lawyers can craft amendments and

74

propose alternative language favorable to your interests.
- Litigation support - In a contract dispute, your lawyer already has context to provide stronger counsel and representation.

Just an hour or two of legal review per agreement can prevent issues and liabilities down the road. The investment is well worth it.

Financial Management for Pet Influencers

Growing an influential and profitable pet brand requires careful financial management. This section outlines best practices in areas like budgeting, accounting, taxes, and planning.

Setting Up Financial Systems

Robust financial processes are crucial from day one when launching your influencer career.

Establishing Separate Business Accounts

Maintaining separate business banking and credit accounts helps track and manage business finances apart from personal. Key actions include:

- Open a dedicated business checking account and credit card.
- Update accounting systems to integrate new accounts.
- Use business accounts exclusively for any pet influencer-related transactions.

Separation provides legal protections and simplifies accounting and taxes.

Utilizing Accounting Software and Tools

Leverage digital accounting systems tailored to influencers to organize expenses, invoices, payments, taxes and more. Popular options include:

- QuickBooks Online - Robust small business accounting software.
- HoneyBook - Specifically designed for solopreneurs and influencers.
- FreshBooks - Cloud accounting platform great for managing invoices.
- Bill.com - Digital payments solution with accounting integration.

Automating as much of your accounting workflow as possible is ideal.

Keeping Accurate Financial Records

Meticulous financial record-keeping prevents headaches come tax time. Best practices include:

- Collecting receipts for ALL business purchases and expenses.
- Creating detailed invoices for each client or campaign.
- Recording income sources and amounts.
- Filing taxes annually - don't let records pile up.
- Retaining documents for a minimum of 7 years.

Err on the side of keeping more records than you think necessary. You'll thank yourself later.

Budgeting and Financial Planning

With income ebb and flow, smart budgeting and planning prevents financial surprises.

Creating a Budget for Your Influencer Activities

A budget provides visibility into where your money comes from and goes. Core elements of an influencer budget include:

- Income – Project your annual earnings from sponsored content, affiliate marketing, licensing fees, etc. Be conservative if your income fluctuates.
- Operating expenses – Budget regular monthly pet care, equipment, software, legal/accounting, and other overhead costs.
- Variable campaign expenses – Estimate costs for things like travel, photography, or gear needed per campaign.
- Marketing investments – Factor in expenses like website hosting, advertising, or brand partnerships to support growth.
- Taxes – Plan for both quarterly estimated payments and annual tax liabilities. The IRS requires you pay taxes on income as its earned.
- Personal draws – Determine a monthly amount you'll take for your living expenses.

Revisit your budget monthly and adjust categories to match evolving realities. Planning goes a long way toward preventing that "where did the money go" feeling.

Planning for Taxes and Unexpected Expenses

Budgeting helps anticipate infrequent but inevitable costs like:

- Emergency vet bills - Pet illness or injuries can lead to multi-thousand dollar vet expenses. Have an emergency fund or pet insurance.
- Equipment failures/replacements - Budget for eventual camera and other equipment upgrades or fix costs.
- Contractors - If hiring help like web developers, photographers etc., allow room in your budget. Their labor can be a significant yet vital investment.
- Quarterly estimated taxes - Determine your expected tax liability and set aside 25% each quarter to avoid underpayment penalties.

Proactively planning for large one-time expenses makes them far less disruptive when they inevitably arise.

Reinvesting Earnings for Growth and Sustainability

Rather than spending your profits, consider reinvesting a portion in your business:

- Build your emergency fund - Gradually grow your reserve funds to 6-12+ months of operating expenses. This provides a buffer for an income downturn.
- Invest in marketing - Allocate budget to advertising, partnerships, SEO, and other growth initiatives.
- Upgrade equipment - Replace outdated cameras, computers, lighting, and software over time.
- Hire support staff - Bring on contractors for assistance with administrative work, content editing, web services etc.
- Fund content creation - Pay for high-quality custom photoshoots, licensed stock content, and unique experiences to create novel content.

Reinvested earnings can amplify your reach and earnings over time through compounding returns.

Tax Considerations for Influencers

Taxes are often the most complex aspect of financial management for pet influencers. Staying compliant and maximizing deductions takes forethought.

Understanding Tax Obligations and Deductions

As a self-employed influencer, you must pay self-employment taxes for Social Security and Medicare along with federal, state and local income taxes. However you can deduct all valid business expenses. Common write-offs include:

- Pet care costs - Food, grooming, vet bills
- Home office expenses - Prorated rent, utilities, internet
- Equipment - Cameras, computers, software, mobile devices
- Travel - Hotels, airfare, mileage for business trips
- Marketing - Advertising, branding, website hosting
- Professional services - Photography/videography, legal, accounting

Thoroughly tracking expenses maximizes your tax deductions and savings.

Keeping Track of Expenses and Income

Using accounting software and a business credit card streamlines the process of pulling tax details. Important practices include:

79

- Save all receipts, invoices, bank/CC statements in your accounting system.
- Categorize transactions to track which are tax deductible business expenses.
- Run profit and loss reports to see your taxable business income for the year.

Having organized records makes filing far less painful.
Seeking Professional Help for Tax Compliance
Hiring a certified tax professional provides experience and expertise that prevents costly errors. A tax preparer can:

- Advise on what expenses are deductible and how to optimize write-offs.
- Ensure you complete all required filings and avoid penalties.
- Spot red flags or issues with your accounting that could trigger an audit.
- Explain complex topics like depreciation, carryover losses, and estimated payments.

Getting personalized tax help tailored to your situation provides peace of mind and optimization.

Risk Management and Insurance

Pet influencers take on various business risks that should be addressed through prudent planning and insurance.

Identifying and Mitigating Risks

Being proactive helps minimize the likelihood and impact of adverse events.

Assessing Risks in Pet Influencing Activities

Common risks spanning financial, operational, legal, and hazard categories include:

Financial

- Income volatility from reliance on sponsorships
- Unexpected slow periods between campaigns
- Large quarterly tax payments

Operational

- Missing content deadlines and damaging relationships
- Platform algorithm changes reducing reach
- Camera/computer failures interrupting workflows

Legal

- Defamation lawsuits from questionable brand partnerships
- Allegations of copyright/trademark infringement
- Hacking of sensitive user account credentials

Hazard

- Pet injuries during travels or photoshoot accidents
- Weather damages during on-location filming
- Auto accidents getting to destinations

Identify risks specific to your particular circumstances and influencer niche.

Developing Strategies to Mitigate Potential Risks

Once risks are assessed, you can get proactive with mitigation strategies:

- Build an emergency fund – This provides a financial cushion in case of lost income or unplanned expenses.
- Diversify income streams – Don't rely solely on a single social platform or small group of brands to avoid over dependency.
- Backup content and data – Store files in multiple locations to prevent losing access in a device failure or hack.
- Plan for delays – Pad schedules and set expectations with partners in case unexpected events slow projects.
- Review insurance policies – Ensure your plans cover potential hazards from travel shoots, equipment damages, or pet injuries.

Taking preventative measures before issues occur leads to better outcomes.

Planning for Emergencies and Contingencies

Develop contingency plans detailing how you will address various emergency scenarios:

- If a pet gets injured, the backup is to post archival photos and notify clients you may miss content deadlines.
- If equipment breaks, rentals provide a short term backup while items get repaired or replaced.
- If you become ill, draft evergreen posts in advance that can auto-publish so your feed stays active.

Having plans ready for likely emergencies lets you handle them smoothly.

Insurance Options for Influencers

The right insurance coverage protects your business assets and mitigates financial risks.

Exploring Insurance Coverage for Pet Influencers

Common insurance needs include:

General liability - Covers legal claims, property damage, or bodily injuries caused by you or your pet to others.

Professional liability - Protects against claims your professional advice or services harmed a client or partner.

Equipment coverage - Pays for repair or replacement of stolen or damaged cameras, computers, drones, etc.

Pet insurance - Offsets veterinary costs for pet injuries or illnesses.

Travel - If filming on-location, travel/event cancellation policies allow you to recover costs from unexpected interruptions.

Assess your specific risks to identify beneficial policies.

Protecting Your Business and Personal Assets

The right insurance limits your financial downside in a range of scenarios:

- General liability insurance helps cover legal defense costs and settlement damages. This provides protection if, for example, your dog bites and injures someone.
- Professional liability limits potential losses if you face claims of failing to deliver on campaign obligations.
- Equipment coverage pays for expensive camera replace-

ments if they are damaged, lost, or stolen.

- Comprehensive travel policies allow you to recoup expenses for interrupted influencer trips.

Review policy limits and exclusions carefully to ensure you have adequate protection.

Navigating Insurance Policies and Claims

Follow best practices when obtaining coverage and submitting claims:

- Work with agents - They help assess risks and align appropriate policy types/limits. Be transparent about your activities.
- Review renewals annually - Update policies to address evolving risks as your business scales.
- Document events - Take detailed records like photos and statements if you need to submit a claim.
- Follow claims procedures - Comply with all required timeframes and forms to receive payouts.
- Get expert help - Consider legal counsel if your claim gets denied and you want to appeal.

Knowing how to properly secure and utilize insurance is critical. Don't wait for a loss before learning best practices.

Planning for the Future

Your influencer career can have incredible longevity if you lay the groundwork for long-term success and sustainability.

Setting Long-Term Financial Goals

84

It's never too soon to think about your long-term objectives and start working backwards:

- Do you want to retire early and if so, when? What income is required?
- Do you aspire to grow into a mega influencer brand or maintain a boutique feel?
- How long do you want to sustain influencer income - until retirement, a few years, indefinitely?
- Does your vision require saving to buy a home, purchase a studio, invest in new venture opportunities?

Setting clear long-term money goals allows you to work methodically towards them.

Preparing for Retirement and Succession

- Calculate your retirement needs - Factor in desired income, healthcare costs, and estimated social security and retirement plan payments to determine any gaps.
- Build passive income - Develop books, online courses, licensing deals and other income that continues even after you stop actively influencing.
- Manage business valuation - Understand what your influencer brand would sell for if you wanted to eventually cash out or transition ownership.
- Define succession plans - Decide if you want to eventually shift creative control to others like selling to employees or partners vs. shutting down entirely.

Putting a retirement and succession roadmap in place provides clarity and direction for the future.

Building a Sustainable Business Model

Striving to create an influencer business with staying power requires avoiding common pitfalls:

- Don't rely too heavily on social platforms - Diversify across channels and own your audience data so you don't lose everything if an algorithm shifts.
- Focus on evergreen content - Trendy topics fade fast. Create content with longer shelf lives.
- Build genuine community - Don't take shortcuts that jeopardize trust with your audience. Maintain integrity above all else.
- Reinvest to evolve - Avoid stagnation by continually experimenting with new content formats, platforms, and streams of revenue.
- Separate personal from business - Keep some semblance of work/life balance and privacy to prevent burnout.

With deliberate mindfulness, pet influencers can build brands that prosper for the long haul.

9

Keeping It Real and Fun

Balancing Business and Pleasure

Launching your pet into social media stardom can be an exciting and rewarding endeavor. However, as their online presence grows, it's important not to lose sight of what matters most - your pet's happiness and wellbeing. Keeping things fun and authentic, both in your content and your relationship with your pet, creates a sustainable path to success.

Prioritizing Your Pet's Happiness

Your pet's comfort and enjoyment should always come first when running a pet influencer business. Pay close attention to their needs and signals to ensure the work you do together aligns with their personality and preferences.

Recognizing Your Pet's Needs and Comfort

Get to know your pet's unique rhythms and boundaries.

Notice when they seem tired, overstimulated, or unhappy. Be prepared to pause or stop shooting photos or videos if your pet shows signs of stress or anxiety. Their health and comfort should be prioritized over capturing the perfect content.

Provide ample time for your pet to rest undisturbed, and don't force them into unfamiliar situations that scare them. Work with your pet's natural energy levels and interests to determine a reasonable content schedule.

Balancing Workload with Playtime and Rest

Make sure your pet has plenty of time for favorite activities, toys, and experiences beyond creating content. Fun adventures together build your bond and recharge you both.

Try to maintain normalcy in their daily routine. Don't let content obligations overwhelm quality time just being a pet. Schedule work in short bursts with breaks, not prolonged periods that exhaust your pet.

Signs of Stress in Pets and How to Address Them

Look for body language or behaviors that may indicate anxiety or unhappiness. Yawning, lip licking, tail tucking, hiding, growling, or unusual agitation can signal stress. If you notice these, stop what you're doing and help your pet calm down.

Address sources of stress for your pet. Consider whether environments, activities, or the amount of content creation are contributing to their discomfort. Make adjustments to ensure their lifestyle stays low-stress.

Maintaining Authenticity in Your Brand

As your pet gains notoriety, stay grounded in who they truly are. Keep your content real and resist the temptation to "stage" unrealistic scenarios. Your pet's authentic personality is what audiences connect with.

Staying True to Your Pet's Personality

Let your pet's distinctive quirks and behaviors drive your content. Don't try to force your pet into content that clashes with their natural preferences. Feature them in ways that feel genuine and unscripted.

Avoid using props or costumes that seem silly or out-of-character just to drive engagement. Focus on capturing your authentic pet, not manufactured personas.

Avoiding Over-Commercialization

While sponsorships may help monetize your pet's fame, resist plugging excessive products just for money. Followers crave authenticity, not constant ads.

Vet potential partnerships to ensure they fit your brand. Reject deals that compromise your pet's image or push products that don't align with their lifestyle.

Ensuring Content Reflects Real Life

Don't filter your feed to portray an unrealistic portrait of a perfect pet. Show real life, including the silly, messy, and mundane moments.

Be open when your pet is having an "off" day. Don't cover up behavior issues or health problems. Followers often relate to the ups and downs of real pet parenthood.

Engaging in Fun and Safe Activities

Explore new pursuits and adventures your pet genuinely enjoys. Let their interests guide public content that entertains audiences while enriching your pet's life.

Finding Activities That Your Pet Enjoys

Experiment to learn which games, sports, outings or enrichment activities get your pet excited. Notice the types of play and environments they naturally gravitate towards.

Incorporate these into your content creation, capturing them doing what they love. Happy pets exude infectious joy that engages followers.

Sharing Joyful Moments with Your Audience

The most popular influencer content features pets doing activities they find intrinsically rewarding. Their obvious enthusiasm and fun is what makes the footage endearing.

Capture your pet's playful essence by letting them lead spontaneous games or adventures. Your video will convey authentic excitement that viewers adore.

Safe and Pet-Friendly Activities for Content

Research unfamiliar activities beforehand to assess safety risks or potential stressors for your pet. Prepare properly to avoid dangerous situations when filming engaging content.

Outdoor adventures require preparation for weather, terrain, hydration, pet-safe plants/water sources, and emergency contingencies. Always put safety first.

Ensuring Your Pet's Well-being

Balancing pet social media success with animal wellness requires vigilance. Monitor their health and comfort closely as their fame grows. Never sacrifice their well-being for profit or popularity.

Health and Safety First

Make your pet's physical health and safety a top priority. Regularly monitor their condition and be vigilant for risks. Address problems promptly.

Regular Health Check-Ups and Care

Schedule well visits to keep vaccinations current and get comprehensive exams. Seek treatment immediately if you notice signs of illness or injury.

Follow veterinary recommendations for preventative care, dental health, nutrition, exercise, grooming, and safety precautions. Keep detailed records of medical history.

Understanding Pet Safety in Various Settings

Research potential hazards in your home, yard, or any new environments you take your pet. Puppy-proof or cat-proof appropriately. Supervise outdoor time.

Use caution introducing pets to props, costumes, or activities. Ensure proper fit and comfort, never impeding movement, vision, breathing, or temperature regulation.

Nutrition and Exercise for Your Pet

Provide species-appropriate nutrition and enrich their routine with adequate exercise and stimuli for optimal health. Activity level may need adjustment if less active during filming.

Adapt these to your pet's changing needs as they age. Monitor for weight gain/loss and adjust caloric intake and exercise accordingly.

Mental and Emotional Health

Your pet can't directly communicate when they feel burnt out or unhappy. Pay close attention to indirect signals. Make sure their psychological needs are met.

Recognizing and Addressing Anxiety or Discomfort

Look for body language, new destructive behaviors, or changes in bathroom habits or social interactions - potential indicators of stress or anxiety needing attention.

If you suspect your pet is unhappy, talk to your veterinarian. Adjust their routine and schedule to avoid activities that trigger stress.

Providing Mental Stimulation and Enrichment

Prevent boredom and frustration by rotating toys, introducing new sights/sounds/smells, and engaging your pet's natural foraging/hunting instincts with food puzzles.

Provide outlets for natural behaviors. Give cats opportunities to scratch, climb, pounce and play hunt. Give dogs chewing toys and chances to dig, herd, and play fetch.

Building a Supportive and Loving Environment

Shower your pet with affection and give them your full attention, free of distractions. Spend one-on-one quality time together.

Ensure they still receive adequate sleep, socialization, play and training. Maintain consistent rules and routines when not creating content.

Handling Fame and Public Attention

As visibility increases, help your pet navigate the effects of their newfound fame to avoid stress. Closely monitor their reactions to ensure celebrity status doesn't detract from their happiness.

Protecting Your Pet from Overexposure

Be selective about public appearances and limit fan interactions to avoid sensory overload for your pet. Schedule adequate downtime between events.

Set boundaries on filming or photo requests to control your pet's exposure. Safeguard their off-duty time fiercely.

Managing Public Interactions and Privacy

Supervise all public encounters with fans to prevent stressful situations. Politely decline if your pet seems uncomfortable interacting with strangers wanting photos or autographs.

Don't share your pet's location publicly when attending events, filming on location, or on vacation. Protect their personal time from disruption.

Coping with the Effects of Fame on Pets

Fame fundamentally changes a pet's lifestyle. Monitor closely for signs of stress adjusting to their new reality. Consult professionals if behavioral problems emerge.

Help your pet cope by providing predictability in scheduling. Maintain pre-fame routines, activities, toys and family time so they retain a sense of normalcy.

Enjoying the Journey Together

The bond between pet and guardian deepens when sharing experiences together. Celebrate your pet's successes, appreciate simple joys, and lay the groundwork for a fulfilling future together.

Celebrating Milestones and Achievements

Mark major moments in your pet's influencer journey with special recognition. Reflect together on how far you've come.

Marking Important Moments in Your Pet's Career

Order a custom cake on their "workiversary" marking petfluencing milestones. Make a big deal of major follower growth with a special treat or adventure.

Display achievements like plaques, play buttons or merchandise prominently in your home to appreciate their progress. Share successes proudly with your community.

Reflecting on Growth and Success

Periodically review your pet's back catalogue of content. Appreciate how much their skills and confidence have progressed thanks to practice and your support.

Highlight growth metrics to remind yourself and followers how significantly your pet's audience has expanded through dedication and authenticity.

Creating Lasting Memories with Your Pet

Capture keepsake photos/videos commemorating meaningful milestones so you'll both have fond memories of shared accomplishments.

Journal about your pet's influencer journey to immortalize special moments. Someday this will become a cherished record of the experiences you had together.

Staying Grounded and Grateful

Amid the whirlwind of pet fame, stay present in each shared moment. Cherish your relationship above all else. Express gratitude.

Appreciating the Bond with Your Pet

No matter how successful your pet becomes, remember that shared love eclipses fame. Deepen your connection through attention, affection and play.

Savor quiet moments together cuddling or participating in favorite routines. Let these serve as calming touchstones amid chaos.

Embracing the Simple Joys of Pet Ownership

Delight in playful antics and everyday interactions that make loving a pet so special, regardless of social media presence. Keep your focus here.

Welcome moments of ordinary fun like chasing string, sharing a treat, or going for a walk. Let these ground you in what truly matters.

Sharing Your Gratitude with Your Audience

Frequently reflect to followers how much your pet enriches your life beyond social media. Express heartfelt appreciation for their role in your family.

Model positive pet relationships for fans. Share tips for strengthening guardian/pet bonds. Spread gratitude for pets as loyal companions.

Planning for a Sustainable Future

A petfluencing career has a limited lifespan. Plan responsibly for retirement and your pet's comfort long-term. Keep building your relationship well after fame fades.

Thinking Long-Term About Your Pet's Career

Research typical career lengths in your petfluencing niche. Have realistic expectations for sustaining fame and revenue. Financially prepare for transitions.

Periodically evaluate whether your pet still enjoys content creation, or shows readiness for retirement. Prioritize their needs over profit.

Preparing for Changes and Transitions

Save adequately for future pet care needs. Expect lifestyle changes like reduced income, more relaxed schedules, and less public visibility after retiring from petfluencing.

Develop new home routines to fill the gaps left by ceased content creation and brand obligations. Explore lower-key hobbies your retired pet may enjoy.

Ensuring a Happy, Fulfilling Life for Your Pet

Commit fully to caring for your pet long after their fame declines. Provide the best nutrition, medical care, enrichment and attention regardless of their celebrity status.

Focus on sustaining a strong bond well into your pet's senior years. Jointly adapt to changing abilities and energy levels as your pet ages.

Final Thoughts: Keeping It Real and Fun

Balancing pet social media success with animal welfare is a major responsibility. Never lose sight of your pet's fundamental needs and preferences. Make their happiness the top priority as you navigate building an authentic brand and creating engaging content audiences love. Commit fully to your pet's health and wellbeing, both during their time in the spotlight and long after. Maintain a strong relationship grounded in real life joy. Ultimately, the love between you is what truly matters.

FAQs: Keeping It Real and Fun

Q: How do I know if petfluencing is right for my pet?

A: Pay close attention to your pet's personality and energy levels. Ensure they enjoy interacting with cameras and crowds. Start slowly and monitor for signs of stress. Be prepared to stop if they indicate discomfort.

Q: What are signs my pet needs a break from petfluencing?

A: Excessive sleeping, hiding, unusual aggression or other behavioral changes can signal burnout. Note decreases in energy/appetite. Stop creating content if your pet shows discomfort.

Q: How much "work" time should pets spend creating content?

A: Limit sessions to a maximum of 30 minutes, a few times weekly, for adult pets. Monitor for fatigue and end immediately if your pet loses interest or energy. Let your pet determine the pace.

Q: How can I make sure sponsorships don't compromise

my pet's brand image?

A: Reject partnerships with brands that don't authentically align with your pet's interests and lifestyle. Be wary of excessive merchandising. Prioritize your pet's reputation.

Q: What are some signs my pet is stressed by their fame?

A: Increased barking, overgrooming, appetite changes, gastrointestinal issues, or destructive behaviors at home may indicate your pet is struggling to cope with their new lifestyle.

10

The Power of Visual Storytelling: Crafting Compelling Visual Content for Pet Influencers

Visual content has become a pivotal part of social media marketing and brand building in the digital age. For pet influencers and brands, impactful visual storytelling can help engage audiences, convey emotions, and build meaningful connections. This comprehensive guide will explore the elements of creating compelling visual content, techniques for engaging audiences, and innovative visual storytelling strategies. Let's dive in and unlock the power of visuals for your pet brand.

Crafting Compelling Visual Content

The foundation of effective visual storytelling is creating compelling, high-quality visual assets. Here are some key considerations when capturing and producing visual content for your pet brand.

Basics of Pet Photography and Videography

To make your pet the star of captivating photos and videos, you need to master some photography and videography basics:

Tips for Capturing High-Quality Images:

- Use natural lighting when possible for clear, vivid photos. Avoid direct harsh sunlight.
- Frame shots creatively to highlight your pet's personality. Get on their eye level.
- Adjust camera settings like aperture and shutter speed to sharpen details and achieve blurring for effect.
- Shoot in RAW format for higher resolution and easier editing.
- Take lots of shots and variety to get some great options.

Understanding Lighting, Composition, and Framing:

- Lighting sets the mood. Direct sun can convey playfulness. Soft light communicates warmth. Silhouettes make dramatic statements.
- Composition is key. The rule of thirds, leading lines, depth of field, and patterns create interest.
- Get creative with framing. Close-ups, wide shots, profiles, and perspectives communicate stories.

Choosing the Right Equipment:

- Invest in a quality DSLR camera and lens suited for pet photography. Go for speed and clarity.

- Use a gimbal or stabilizer for smooth videography. A shotgun mic improves audio quality.
- Consider drones or action cams for unique aerial shots and activity footage.
- Ensure adequate memory cards and batteries for extensive shoots.

With practice and the right gear, you can consistently create pro-quality pet visual content.

Telling Stories Through Visuals

Great pet photography isn't just about capturing cute moments. The most compelling visuals use strategic elements to tell captivating stories about your pet:

Conveying Emotions and Narratives:

- Showcase your pet's personality through joyful romps, silly antics, restful naps, and more.
- Photograph sequences and rituals that capture the spirit of your pet's daily life and relationships.
- Videography can showcase behaviors, quirks, and changes over time.

Thematic and Stylistic Choices:

- Coordinate outfits, backdrops, and props to create cohesive sets and aesthetics.
- Use lighting, composition, effects, and editing for unity across images and videos.
- Develop original concepts, get creative with unique an-

gles, and infuse your perspective.

Creating a Visual Brand Signature:

- What makes your pet and content unique? Reflect that in styling choices.
- Establish a consistent look, feel, and quality for recognition.
- Include subtle branded elements like logos and color schemes for consistency.

By applying strategic and creative techniques, you can craft visual content that engages audiences and builds your brand identity.

Editing and Enhancing Visuals

The editing process can transform good visuals into great ones ready to captivate your audience.

Basic Editing Techniques:

- Adjust lighting, temperature, vibrance, and clarity.
- Crop and straighten lines for compelling compositions.
- Seamlessly remove distractions and blemishes.
- Fine-tune focus and accentuate details.

Using Filters and Effects:

- Subtle filters like "Ludwig" can add mood. Dramatic ones like "Valencia" make statements.
- When appropriate, play with effects like light leaks, lens

flares, vignettes, and textures.

- Use judiciously. Filters shouldn't overwhelm or look gimmicky.

Polishing Tools and Apps:

- Mobile apps like Snapseed, Adobe Lightroom, or VSCO offer robust editing options.
- Invest in professional software like Adobe Photoshop and Premiere for precision.
- Enlist a graphic designer or editing service for an expert polish.

Mindful editing takes visual assets to the next level so they captivate audiences and align with your brand style.

Engaging Your Audience with Visuals

It's not enough to just create high-quality visuals. You need to produce content tailored to engage your audience.

Creating Interactive Visual Content

Rather than passively viewing images, you can provide ways for fans to interact, creating a more immersive experience:
Incorporating User Interaction:

- Enable image comments to start conversations.
- Use relevant hashtags so fans can discover your posts.
- Add swipe up or link in bio connections to drive traffic.
- Incorporate built-in interactive elements like polls, Q&As

and sliders.

Leveraging Visuals for Contests:

- Photo contests that encourage user submissions and hashtags drive awareness.
- Creative video challenges like pet talent shows provide entertaining participation opportunities.

Encouraging User-Generated Content:

- Share user photos of their pets interacting with your products.
- Spotlight the best fan art and content featuring your brand.
- Repost the most engaging visual content created by your audience.

Interactive elements make visuals more participatory. Audiences crave that experience.

The Role of Visuals in Branding

Compelling, consistent visuals are also vital for reinforcing what your pet brand represents.

Building an Aesthetic:

- Determine the look that embodies your brand (rustic, elegant, fun, etc).
- Curate feed visuals that bring that aesthetic to life.
- Coordinate branded merchandise, packaging, and mar-

keting to match.

Consistency and Variation:

- Maintain recognizable stylistic and tonal elements across visual content.
- Also create fresh, novel images and videos to maintain interest.

Visual Brand Recognition:

- Unique props, logos, color schemes, and locations become associated with your brand.
- Fans will recognize your posts instantly when flipping through feeds.
- This trains audiences to seek out and trust your brand.

Strategic visuals boost brand awareness, loyalty, and engagement over time.

Maximizing Impact on Different Platforms

To maximize reach, you need to tailor visuals based on the unique aspects of key social platforms.
Optimizing for Specific Platforms:

- Square 1:1 images and Stories stand out on Instagram.
- Vertical video thrives on TikTok. Landscape video dominates YouTube.
- Multi-image posts perform well on Facebook. Limit text and emojis.

- Consider content duration, sound, branding, and community expectations.

Cross-Platform Strategies:

- Repurpose video clips as Reels. Turn top-performing vertical assets into horizontal formats.
- Adapt still images into short videos with movement, music, or effects.
- Ensure consistent editing, filters, logos, captions and hashtags.

Analyzing Performance:

- Compare engagement and growth across platforms. Double down on what resonates.
- Poll followers on preferred platforms and content styles.
- Refine platform-specific strategies over time based on data.

Keep testing visual content tailored to each platform's specialties and culture.

Visual Storytelling Techniques

Moving beyond individual images and videos, you can employ narrative techniques and emotional engagement strategies to take your visual storytelling to the next level.

Narrative Techniques in Visuals

Visual story arcs keep audiences hooked and invested in your pet's journey over the long term.

Crafting Story Arcs:

- Serialize changes like your pet growing up through mile-stone images.
- Build suspense and anticipation for big reveals like pregnancy or adoption news.
- Showcase amusing sequences like learning a new trick.

Conveying Personality and Lifestyle:

- Bring your pet to life through recurring motifs that capture their quirks.
- Feature "day in the life" videos highlighting charming rituals.
- Showcase your pet exploring favorite hangouts and haunts.

Captions:

- Captions should continue the narrative, not just describe the visuals.
- Share thoughts in your pet's voice for a fun, engaging perspective.
- Use captions to provide endearing backstories and inside jokes.

Through playful narratives over time, audiences become

invested in your pet.

Emotional Engagement Through Visuals

Photos and videos that trigger emotional reactions help fans connect with your pet on a deeper level.
Evoking Emotions:

- Warmth - tender moments of bonding and affection capture hearts.
- Excitement - energetic romps and playtime antics generate thrill.
- Humor - silly situations and antics create amusement.
- Triumph - depictions of growth and new milestones inspire.

Making Connections:

- Help pet parents relate through shared experiences like vet visits or training challenges.
- Feature fan submitted visuals of their own pets interacting with yours.
- Spotlight rescue stories and adoption journeys to drive support for causes.

Balancing Emotions:

- Don't solely post happy, cute, or funny content. Show real life too.
- Address important issues like health conditions when appropriate.

- Authentic vulnerability fosters trust and community.

Images that evoke emotional reactions help deepen audience connection with your pet brand.

Innovating with Visual Content

As trends evolve and new platforms emerge, you need to continually experiment and evolve your visual content approaches.

Experimenting with New Visual Formats:

- Explore emergent social media formats like livestreams or augmented reality effects.
- Breathe new life into static posts with embedded video elements.
- Test out fresh editing styles, filters, transitions, and text/graphic overlays.

Staying Ahead of Trends:

- Observe techniques used by top brands and rising pet influencers.
- Immerse yourself in platform-specific visual communities to spot emerging trends.
- Strike a balance between trendy and timeless so content ages well.

Adapting Strategies:

- Cycle out played out visual tropes and stale styles over

time.

- Double down on approaches that generate spikes in engagement.
- Keep innovating to maintain an edge as a visual content creator.

Consistent evolution ensures your visual storytelling stays fresh, engaging, and effective long-term.

Final Thoughts: Maximizing the Power of Visual Storytelling

For pet influencers and brands, crafting compelling visual content and embracing innovative visual storytelling strategies is essential. Visually capturing your pet's unique personality allows audiences to make emotional connections and become invested in your pet's journey over time. Pairing engaging visuals with strategic narratives, interactivity, and innovation enables you to captivate pet lovers across social media platforms. With these tips and techniques, you're ready to unlock the immense power of visual storytelling and take your pet brand to the next level.

FAQs About Pet Visual Storytelling

What makes strong visual content for pet brands?

Great pet visuals are high-quality, on-brand, engaging, and emotionally evocative while showcasing your pet's personality and lifestyle. Interactive elements and narrative techniques further boost impact.

How can I create on-theme visuals consistently?

Determine a signature style and aesthetic for your pet brand. Coordinate props, backdrops, effects, and editing to ensure cohesion across visuals over time.

What are some low-budget visual storytelling options?

You can tell great stories through iPhone photos and videos. Natural lighting, cute scenarios, and strategic captions go a long way. Get creative editing with free apps.

How do I improve my pet photography skills?

Practice frequently, watch online tutorials, learn your camera settings, understand lighting principles, and invest in some entry-level gear like a 50mm "nifty fifty" lens. Master composition.

What makes an effective visual brand strategy?

Unique, recognizable visual branding you implement across platforms and marketing materials consistently over time. Signature colors, logos, props, styles, and editing define your look.

11

The Art of Writing Captivating Captions: Crafting Text That Enhances Your Visual Content

In the social media world, captions make or break your posts. While compelling images and videos provide the core visual interest, the accompanying text brings the content to life. This guide will explore caption writing techniques to enhance engagement, storytelling, and branding for pet influencers and businesses. Let's unlock the art of crafting captivating captions.

The Art of Caption Writing

Writing effective captions requires skill and strategy. Here are some key principles for creating captivating text to pair with your visual assets.

Elements of a Captivating Caption

Great captions instantly grab attention while providing context and personality.

Balancing Brevity with Information:

- Convey the core message succinctly in the first 1-2 sentences.
- Elaborate with additional intriguing or humorous details.
- Avoid lengthy blocks of text that users won't read.

Infusing Personality:

- Establish a unique tone and perspective. First person works well.
- Share amusing anecdotes, funny quips, or heartfelt thoughts.
- Let your pet's personality shine through with quotes in their voice.

Writing Techniques:

- Use conversational language, creative wording, evocative phrases, and descriptive details.
- Employ literary devices like alliteration, idioms, repetition, and contrasts.
- Vary sentence structure and avoid one-note dryness.

With practice, you can find your captivating caption voice.

Matching Captions with Visuals

Captions should complement and enhance visual content instead of just describing it plainly.
   Creating Harmony:

- Text and visuals together should convey a unified message or mood.
- Use visual cues like color schemes in images to inspire word choices.

Contextualizing:

- Provide relevant backstory, location details, subject identities, etc.
- Clarify ambiguous elements that aren't clear in the visuals alone.

Cross-Platform Variations:

- Longer captions work well on Facebook and Instagram. Be very concise on Twitter.
- YouTube descriptions can incorporate rich metadata and keywords.
- Tailor formatting and style based on platform norms.

Matching brings cohesion to text and visuals for maximum impact.

Captions for Different Purposes

Caption content and style should align with your goals for each post.
Educational vs. Entertaining:

- Informational posts may require more factual details and instructions.
- Humorous posts need witty jokes or amusing observations.

Promotional vs Organic:

- Promotional captions clearly highlight product features and value.
- Organic captions focus on providing value through inspiration or entertainment.

Engagement:

- Ask questions and solicit opinions to spark conversation.
- Share personal anecdotes followers connect with.
- Use CTAs strategically to drive likes, comments, shares, and clicks.

Matching caption style to your goals further enhances messaging and impact.

Enhancing Engagement with Captions

Beyond informative and entertaining content, captions can actively encourage interaction and community building.

Encouraging Interaction

conversational, inclusive captions inspire audiences to engage.

Asking Questions:

- Pose thoughtful questions to spark meaningful discussions in comments.
- Fun polls and surveys also garner responses.

Soliciting Opinions:

- "What do you think of this outfit on Coco?"
- "Doesn't this view look heavenly?"

Direct Engagement:

- "Tag a friend who would love this hike!"
- "Like this pic if delicious treats are your weakness too!"

Well-crafted questions and prompts get audiences actively participating.

Storytelling Through Captions

Using captions to narrate adventures and share insights turns followers into invested fans.
Narrating Experiences:

- Let fans follow along your pet's life story over time.
- Feature memorable misadventures, funny mishaps, and heartwarming moments.

Behind-the-Scenes:

- Give sneak peeks into your creative process, daily rituals, or big projects.
- Pull back the curtain to showcase the hard work behind the scenes.

Broader Connections:

- Relate specific anecdotes to universal themes and senti-ments.
- Find the emotional core that resonates with followers' own lives.

Storytelling captions forge deeper bonds between pets and fans.

Utilizing Humor and Emotion

Captions packed with humor, heart, and humanity work magic.

Humorous Captions:

- Charm fans with amusing observations, silly jokes, funny hashtags, and witty quips.
- Make sure humor aligns with your brand voice.

Emotional Captions:

- Share poignant reflections, profound gratitude, heart-warming delight, and hard-earned lessons.
- Celebrate meaningful milestones, big and small.

Thoughtful Balance:

- Don't rely solely on humor or sentimentality. Vary your tone.
- Occasional heavier topics can resonate when handled with care. Let your authenticity shine through.

Touching hearts and tickling funny bones - that's the caption sweet spot.

Writing for Brand Promotion

When done skillfully, captions can spread brand awareness while still captivating audiences with value and entertainment.

Crafting Promotional Captions

Blend promotional messaging smoothly into engaging captions.

Seamless Integration:

- Briefly mention your product or service contextually. Don't overtly sell.
- Share how offerings enhance your pet's life organically.

Sponsored Post Captions:

- Spotlight sponsor's offerings as solutions relevant to your audience.
- Align sponsored messages with your pet's natural interests and voice.

Balancing Promotion:

- Limit promotional content to 20% of captions or less.
- Surround each sponsored post with multiple entertaining organic posts.

A light touch with promotion maintains trust and loyalty.

SEO Considerations

Optimizing captions for SEO and discovery helps attract new audiences.

Keyword Integration:

- Research relevant long-tail keywords using Google's auto-complete suggestions.
- Organically incorporate keywords based on your post topic.

Social Media SEO Basics:

- Include important keywords early in captions.
- Leverage hashtags, locations, and profile tags for discoverability.

Optimizing for Search:

- Enhance contextual signals like keyword density and relevance.
- captions directly influence how images appear in visual search results.

SEO-enhanced captions expand your pet brand's reach and visibility.

Continuous Improvement

Analyze performance data and evolving trends to keep leveling up your caption skills.
Analyzing Engagement:

- Compare likes and comments across different caption styles and topics.
- Identify your top-performing captions to inform future approaches.

Responding to Feedback:

- Notice which kinds of posts elicit the most compliments or requests for more.
- Adapt your style based on constructive criticism.

Updated Techniques:

- Study caption writing from pet influencers at the top of their game.
- Learn emerging trends like using collaborative captions or leveraging localization.
- Refresh your captions with new concepts so you don't get stale.

Striving for continuous caption improvement ensures your writing stays engaging.

Final Thoughts on Writing Captivating Captions

Captions make the difference between forgettable visuals and unforgettable social media moments with your audience. Tailor text to be informative, on-brand, emotional, humorous, conversational, strategic, and discoverable. Pair engaging captions seamlessly with compelling pet photos and videos to take your content to the next level. With these caption writing tips, you now have an arsenal of techniques for crafting visual social media posts that stop scrollers in their tracks and leave a lasting impact.

FAQs About Captions for Pet Influencers

How long should my social media captions be?

Aim for 2-5 concise sentences or 30-150 characters. Provide essential context and intrigue fans to engage further. Avoid excessive blocks of text.

What makes a good Instagram caption vs a Tweet?

Instagram captions can tell a story or provoke emotions. Tweets should be very compact - think one clever line or prompt.

How do I make promotional content sound natural?

Quickly mention your brand, product, or service contextually. Focus most of the caption on entertaining or informing audiences without overt sales pitches.

What type of captions generate the most engagement?

Captions that spark discussion through questions, encourage sharing, evoke emotion, provide value, or reveal something new tend to see high engagement. Test different styles.

How often should hashtags be used in captions?

1-5 varied, relevant hashtags help with discovery. Avoid hashtag spam that detracts from your caption voice and flow. Monitor performance to find your optimal balance.

12

Expanding Your Pet's Social Media Reach

Gone are the days when having an Instagram account with a few cute pet photos was enough to gain a social media following. In today's oversaturated market, pet influencers need robust multi-platform strategies to stand out and continue growing their personal brands.

Utilizing Multi-Platform Strategies

A key technique for expanding a pet influencer's reach is leveraging multiple social media platforms. Relying solely on one channel significantly limits potential growth. By embracing a diverse mix of platforms, influencers can access expanded audiences and increase visibility.

Embracing Various Social Media Platforms

Certain platforms lend themselves better to pet influencer content than others. Analyzing each channel's unique features and target demographics is crucial for determining an optimal multi-platform approach.

For pet influencers, the core platform is typically Instagram. Its visual nature makes it ideal for sharing high-quality pet photos and videos, which tend to perform well. However, branching out to other major channels like Facebook, YouTube, and TikTok can provide access to untapped audiences.

Facebook's Groups feature gives influencers a place to build engaged online communities around their pets. Pet owners tend to be highly active in Facebook Groups where they can socialize with fellow pet lovers. Leveraging Groups allows influencers to establish themselves as thought leaders while getting valuable user-generated content.

YouTube presents expanded video capabilities beyond Instagram and TikTok. Longer-form vlogs and tutorials resonate strongly with pet owners seeking to enrich their pets' lives. YouTube also enables influencers to establish deeper connections with audiences.

TikTok's short-form viral videos excel at driving growth. The platform's algorithm makes it easier to amass follows fast. Posting pet-centric TikToks that align with trending audios or hashtags can gain quick traction. However, shallow engagement is common. Balancing genuine connection and viral appeal is key.

While smaller platforms like Twitter or Pinterest have limited utility for pet influencers, they remain worth maintaining a presence on. Having accounts on all major networks ensures influencers appear in searches and are discoverable. But platforms lacking visual emphasis or pet-focused users should not be over-prioritized.

Cross-Promotion Techniques

Gaining followings across multiple platforms requires cross-promoting content across profiles. Pointing audiences from one network to another enables tapping into new groups organically.

Posting TikToks natively on Instagram as Reels is an excellent way to showcase content. TikTok videos tend to perform well once repurposed as Instagram Reels. Adding a swipe up link or profile tags connects viewers to the original TikTok account. The same technique works for YouTube Shorts.

Influencers can cross-promote via Instagram Stories by sharing YouTube videos or linking to TikTok and encouraging followers to check them out. Quick behind-the-scenes clips work well for driving interest.

Leveraging linkable platforms like Linktree provides one central hub connecting all accounts. It allows showcasing the variety of platforms used.

Following relevant hashtags on each platform and consistently interacting with that niche community boosts visibility. Engaging with similar pet influencers exposes one's brand to untapped audiences already passionate about pet content.

Consistency Across Platforms

While tailoring content to fit each platform's style is important, maintaining a consistent brand identity across all channels is equally crucial. Audiences that discover a pet influencer on multiple networks should feel they are engaging with one cohesive brand, not multiple disjointed entities.

Profile aesthetics including color schemes, logos, and bios should align across platforms. A recognizable look, feel, and voice unifies accounts into one brand identity.

Hashtags should also carry over to increase discoverability. For example, always including #TheFluffyPups on dog photos brands the content.

Content themes should reflect the brand's core focus. For instance, pet toy reviews should appear on YouTube, Instagram, and TikTok to reinforce the review theme.

Finally, branded assets like logo stickers should overlay videos. Seeing the same sticker on Instagram and TikTok fosters familiarity.

While tailoring content style to fit each platform is good, the heart of the brand and messaging must remain consistent.

Harnessing the Power of Analytics

Analytics provide pet influencers data-driven insights for assessing content performance and identifying new growth opportunities. Regularly analyzing platform analytics is crucial for expanding reach.

Understanding Analytics for Growth

Each platform offers its own analytics, from Instagram Insights to YouTube Studio. Regularly delving into the data identifies what content resonates best.

Key metrics to analyze include:

- Follower growth: Are total followers increasing steadily over time? Sudden drops or plateaus signal issues.
- Reach and impressions: How far is content spreading? Higher numbers indicate good discoverability.
- Engagement rate: Are followers engaging enough? High rates signal captivated audiences.
- Traffic sources: Where do visits originate? This shows which networks/posts drive traffic.
- Audience demographics: What are followers' ages, locations, gender? This enables better understanding one's niche.
- Top performing content: Which posts earn the most engagement and shares? This reveals what content to create more of.

Monitoring analytics over time depicts trends and opportunities. Knowing the audience and their preferences is essential for growth.

Applying Insights to Content Strategy

Analytics offer more than data; they provide actionable insights for capitalizing on successes.

Noticing certain post types consistently have higher en-

127

gagement can inform content calendars. If pet toy unboxings perform well across platforms, planning more unboxing videos is smart.

Seeing traffic spike from a viral TikTok indicates opportunities for expanding into TikTok. Riding trends at the right time seizes growth.

Discovering the majority of followers are 18-24 females guides platforms to focus on. Tailoring content and partnerships to appeal to that demographic helps growth.

If engagement rates decline, re-evaluating content style may be needed or switching up types of posts. Analyzing data uncovers issues.

Essentially, routinely assessing analytics and applying learnings to optimize content strategy is key for sustainable growth.

Tracking Progress and Making Adjustments

Growth requires tracking analytics regularly and making ongoing optimizations based on lessons learned.

Setting monthly goals for follower growth or engagement rates helps benchmark progress. If rates fall below goals, pomoting more aggressively or trying new content formats may help get back on track.

Consistently tracking top traffic sources indicates which platforms drive the most growth. Focusing effort on those high-converting networks pays dividends.

Comparing metrics month over month spotlights trends. For example, seeing TikTok's referral traffic growing could signify its increasing importance to prioritize.

Being flexible and willing to shift gears keeps growth

momentum strong. If Pinterest referrals decline, reallocating time to better-performing platforms is smart.

Ongoing analysis, adjustment, and improvement is integral for any marketing strategy. Savvy pet influencers continually evolve their approaches based on data-backed insights. No growth strategy remains stagnant for long.

Engaging with the Pet Influencer Community

Expanding reach requires engaging with fellow pet influencers through cross-promotion, collaborations, and community building. Tapping into each other's audiences expands reach.

Building Relationships with Fellow Influencers

Developing relationships with other pet influencers fosters growth opportunities. Introducing one's brand to similar influencers can earn cross-promotions while forging connections.

Ways to connect include:

- Commenting regularly on their content with value-adding remarks
- Responding to their Instagram stories or tweets
- Direct messaging complimenting their work
- Partnering for giveaways
- Featuring their account on one's own page

The key is consistently interacting, networking, and demonstrating shared interests. Eventual collaborations may arise.

Pet owners with smaller followings can still be powerful allies. Micro-influencers have highly engaged niches. Gifting products to them or being featured on their pages expands reach.

Influencers with similar content and values tend to gladly cross-promote others. A rising tide lifts all boats. However, spam outreach should be avoided.

Collaborating for Mutual Growth

Strategic collaborations between mutually beneficial pet influencers spark new growth opportunities through expanded reach.

Effective collaborations could include:

- Co-creating content together such as joint reviews, day-in-the-life videos, or vlogs.
- Featuring each other's pets prominently on both accounts through guest appearances.
- Instagram takeovers allowing influencers to showcase pets on each other's accounts.
- Co-hosted giveaways where each promotes the other's products/brand to shared audiences.
- Influencer "families" that regularly create content together.
- Promoting each other's products through gifted reviews and affiliate links.

The crossover exposure from collaborating provides built-in access to new audiences already passionate about pets. Ensuring the collaboration aligns well with both brands' identities is key.

Participating in Online Pet Communities

Engaging actively with online groups like subreddits, Facebook groups, forums etc. related to one's niche provides community-building opportunities while expanding reach.

Joining pet parenting groups and providing value through comments builds goodwill. Pet owners often share influencer recommendations within communities.

Posting pet photos within niche groups leads to direct engagement. Users may discover and follow pages they resonate with.

Hosting "Ask Me Anything" sessions within online communities offers helpful expertise while humanizing the brand.

Running free pet product giveaways exclusive to group members incentivizes following. Small groups still provide high-quality leads.

Being a thoughtful contributor and community member paves the way for word-of-mouth referrals. These organically grown connections foster loyalty.

Remember - pets unite people. Tapping into that directly through online groups cultivates an audience.

Final Thoughts: Multi-Platform Strategies Are Key for Pet Influencer Growth

In an increasingly noisy social media space, multi-platform presences provide needed amplification for pet influencers to stand out from the pack. An integrated approach across selected platforms aligns with how users digest content today.

Audiences should be engaged across their preferred networks through tailored content and cross-promotion. Data-driven insights derived from analytics guide content optimizations over time. And collaborating strategically with mutually beneficial influencers expands reach through built-in audiences.

Most importantly, pet influencers must deliver value on social platforms through authenticity, knowledge and consistent entertainment. Social media may have provided the tools for growth, but genuine pet passion remains the heart.

Frequently Asked Questions

What are the best social media platforms for pet influencers?

Instagram, Facebook, YouTube, and TikTok have the most potential currently. Instagram works well for photos, YouTube for longer videos, Facebook for community and TikTok for fun viral content.

How much time should be spent cross-promoting content daily?

Aim for consistently cross-promoting new posts across platforms over a 1-2 hour window. Re-sharing older high-performing posts daily also helps.

What is the best way to track analytics?

Using social media management tools like Hootsuite provides a unified dashboard to efficiently track key metrics across platforms. Reviewing insights weekly in a tool is ideal.

How often should I post on each platform?

Posting once daily is a solid goal on Instagram, Facebook and TikTok. For YouTube 2-3x a week works well. Tailor based on analytics but consistency is key.

What makes an effective influencer collaboration?

Aligning with someone in your niche with similar audiences but minimal overlap maximizes cross-promotion opportunities. Ensure your personal brands mesh well too.

13

Creative Content Creation for Pet Influencers

As a pet influencer, your content is the lifeblood of your channel. Creating unique, engaging content consistently is key to growing and maintaining an audience in the saturated world of social media. With so many pet accounts vying for attention, it's vital to think outside the box and develop innovative content ideas to stand out.

This chapter will explore creative ideation, aesthetics and branding, and utilizing storytelling techniques to produce shareworthy pet content that sparks joy and makes meaningful connections.

Innovative Content Ideas

Coming up with new content ideas as a pet influencer can be challenging. However, taking inspiration from trending topics, seasons, and your pet's personality are great starting points for brainstorming.

Brainstorming Unique Concepts

Don't limit yourself to the obvious pet content like cute photos and videos. Here are some innovative types of content to create:

- Pet product reviews - Make entertaining and informative videos testing out the latest pet gadgets, toys, or gear. Vox-style videos work well for concise reviews.
- Pet DIY tutorials - Guide viewers through crafting toys, treats, costumes, or accessories for their pets with step-by-step tutorials. DIY contests can also engage your audience.
- Petcare education - Create informational content like tips for training, healthcare, nutrition, and more. Infographics and listicles work well for concise education.
- Pet styling and grooming - Showcase trendy pet hairstyles, nail art, creative grooming, and fashionable accessories.
- Cooking videos - Whip up healthy recipes and fun treats for pets like pupcakes, "pawcakes", frozen treats, and more.
- Pet fitness - Share exercise tips, workout routines, sports training, and activities to keep pets fit.
- Pet hacks - Demonstrate clever solutions to common pet care problems with easy, affordable DIY hacks.
- Vlogs and vlogging - Give fans a peek into a day in the life of your pet through video blogs and vlogs. Capture your pet's daily adventures.
- Pet advice - Offer useful tips and advice about pet care as a knowledgeable influencer. Share your experience and

expertise.

The key is creating content that provides value to your audience while highlighting your pet's unique personality. Take inspiration from trends but put your own spin on them.

Seasonal and Trending Content Ideas

Creating topical content tied to seasons, holidays, and trends will help attract new viewers while delighting your current audience.

Some seasonal content ideas include:

- Spring - Easter photo shoots, flower crowns, spring cleaning tips, seasonal allergies info.
- Summer - Pool parties, beach trips, road trips, camping adventures, summer safety.
- Fall - Back to school content, Halloween costumes, fall foliage trips, Thanksgiving treats.
- Winter - Holiday outfits, Christmas card shoots, winter activities, New Year's Eve treats.

You can also tap into trending topics and themes to create timely content, such as:

- Pop culture - Recreate popular movie scenes or memes. Do pet versions of viral Internet challenges.
- Current events - Make educational content around awareness months/days or news events related to pets.
- Viral products - Review hot trending pet products and toys. Recreate viral food recipes.

- Hashtags - Jump on trending story and challenge hashtags like #WearEmWednesday.

Stay active on social media and check trending lists to spot opportunities for creating topical content.

Creating Series and Recurring Themes

Developing a series creates anticipation and keeps viewers returning for more. Recurring themes also helps build your brand identity.

Some ideas for series or themes include:

- "Wacky Wednesday" - Dress up in wacky costumes every Wednesday.
- "Trick of the Week" - Teach a new fun trick or skill each week.
- "Toy Tester" - Review a new toy every month.
- "Paw-trait Artist" - Paint paintings with your paws monthly.
- "Battle of the Breeds" - Compare pros and cons of different breeds.
- "PAW-STARS" - Recreate famous movie/TV scenes.
- "Fashion Hauls" - Model seasonal pet fashion looks.

Having planned content buckets gives you room for spontaneity while keeping content creation consistent. Repurpose themes into playlists, highlight reels, and shorts too.

Visual Aesthetics and Branding

Developing a strong visual aesthetic and on-brand content style bolsters recognition and loyalty. Keep your content consistent and aligned with your pet's personality.

Developing a Signature Style

Determine a visual style and vibe that fits your pet influencer brand. Stay consistent with colors, fonts, editing techniques, and overall tone.

Some elements that comprise your visual style:

- Color palette - Choose a consistent color scheme and filters that reflect your brand.
- Fonts - Select complementary fonts for your thumbnails, graphics, and overlays.
- Tone - Decide on an overall style - playful, elegant, funky, minimal, retro, modern, etc.
- Graphic elements - Design graphics, stickers, frames, etc. to brand your content.
- Editing - Develop signature editing techniques like slow motion, music, text animations.
- Thumbnails - Create eye catching yet on-brand thumbnails using bold text, high contrast, and vibrant imagery.

Testing different aesthetics will help you identify what resonates most with your audience and pet's persona. Lean into this style.

Consistency in Visual Presentation

While experimenting is good, consistency is key for a strong brand identity. Use templates and branding elements to maintain a steady style.

Ways to create consistent visuals:

- Develop content templates with your branding, logo, color scheme and graphics built in.
- Use the same intro/outro sequence. Create a signature intro for your YouTube videos.
- Add branded borders, frames or watermarks to photos and videos.
- Stick to one dominant color scheme. Use the same selective coloring techniques.
- Be consistent with filter types and editing style.
- Use branded graphics, stickers, animations, and text highlights.
- Maintain steady thumbnails and title styles.

Having set assets, templates, and guidelines will streamline creating professional, recognizable content.

Branding and Visual Identity

Align your content with your desired brand identity. Let your pet's personality shine through.

Ways to develop a strong identity through content:

- Showcase your pet's unique quirks and characteristics – Let your pet's natural charm and spirit show. Highlight

their personality.
- Have a consistent "voice" - Maintain the same tone, point of view, and style across videos.
- Respond to comments in-character - Reply in your pet's voice to further personify your brand.
- Share your origin story - Let your audience get to know you through intro videos and about me sections.
- Create merch and products - Design branded merch that fans can proudly wear and share.
- Leverage cameo and speaking opportunities - Accept relevant opportunities to share your brand story.

Staying true to who your pet is will allow you to build an authentic connection with your audience. Let their personality shine in a way that feels genuine, not exaggerated.

Storytelling Through Pet Content

Storytelling gives your content depth. Use compelling narratives to engage your audience. Educate and entertain them through your pet's adventures.

Crafting Engaging Stories

Well-crafted narratives add interest to your pet content. Use stories to tug at the heartstrings, inspire, and mesmerize your viewers.

Storytelling Tips:

- Establish a narrative - Set the scene. Introduce characters, settings, and conflict.

- Build tension and stakes - Create rising action. Use suspense and anticipation.
- Weave in details - Share sights, sounds, thoughts. Build emotional connections.
- Reach a climax - Hit a high point of tension or action.
- Resolve the tension - Release suspense and resolve central conflict.
- Close with a reflection - End with a meaningful thought or revelation.
- Use natural dialog and first-person - Share direct thoughts and conversational moments to pull the viewer into the action.
- Add b-roll - Use supplemental footage and photos to illustrate the story.

Stories add three-dimensionality and drama that pulls viewers in. Vlog daily moments through a narrative lens.

Using Narratives to Connect with Audiences

Stories allow you to bond with viewers on a deeper level. Sharing challenges and triumphs fosters a personal connection.
Ways to use storytelling for engagement:

- Share your origin story - Let viewers get to know how you met your pet and started your influencer journey.
- Open up about vulnerabilities - Be honest about struggles and hardships you face with empathetic storytelling.
- Feature milestone moments - Capture your pet's adventures like first birthdays, new tricks learned, big trips, etc.

- Talk about relationships and friendships - Show warm interactions with family, friends, significant others, and fans.
- Discuss pet care challenges - Share stories of health scares, injuries, or conditions needing treatment.
- Highlight acts of heroism - Feature pets who saved the day by alerting owners of danger, stopping crimes, rescuing people, etc.
- Celebrate underdog comebacks - Share uplifting stories of disadvantaged, disabled, or special needs pets overcoming challenges.

Vulnerability and triumph stories foster supportive communities while spotlighting important issues.

Balancing Education and Entertainment

Viewers are drawn in by entertainment but also want to learn. Use engaging narratives to seamlessly educate and delight your audience.

Tips for balancing education and entertainment:

- Teach through story - Share educational moments like training successes as part of a compelling recap.
- Use humor and heart - Entertain even in instructional videos. Include bloopers and funny Pet fails.
- Keep it short - Opt for concise videos under 5 minutes to maximize engagement for how-tos.
- Get creative with graphics - Use text overlays, graphics, and b-roll in educational content.
- Go behind the scenes - Give a glimpse of the work and

research that goes into informational content.

- Respond to viewer requests - Address burning questions from your audience in educational content.
- Share personal experiences - Include your own stories and anecdotes when educating about pet care topics.
- Promote discussion - Ask follow-up questions to spark conversation around key lessons.

Finding the sweet spot between education and entertainment takes experimentation. Observe which instructional style best fits your brand.

Final Thoughts: Creative Content Creation

Creating novel, captivating content is key for pet influencers to engage audiences in a cluttered social media landscape. Take inspiration from trending topics but put your unique spin on them. Develop a consistent visual style and brand identity that shines through in all content. And use compelling narratives and storytelling to form meaningful bonds with your viewers. With consistent ideation and experimentation, you can produce inspiring content that spreads joy. The path to originality requires embracing the unknown, breaking from convention, and unafraid to challenge preconceived notions in pursuit of connection. It's a journey of courage, not comfort - are you ready?

FAQs About Creative Pet Influencer Content

What should you avoid when creating pet influencer content?

Avoid dangerous stunts, exotic animal exploitation, overt product pushing, and low-quality, repetitive content. Prioritize your pet's well-being and producing value for viewers.

How can I come up with content ideas easily?

Take inspiration from trending topics on social media, seasonal events, current news, viewer requests, your pet's personality, and your own experiences. Pinterest and forums like Reddit can provide inspiration too.

What makes an effective pet influencer thumbnail?

Effective thumbnails use high contrast colors, bold text, intriguing imagery of your pet, dynamic posing, and consistent branding. Tools like Canva can help create polished thumbnails.

Should I schedule out pet influencer content in advance?

Yes, having a content calendar helps you plan out ideas and creation in advance for consistent posting. Schedule posts at optimal times and promote future content to build anticipation.

How important is video editing for pet influencers?

High-quality editing with transitions, text, graphics, b-roll, and music helps videos stand out. Invest time into learning editing basics like jump cuts, color correcting, text animation, etc.

14

Mastering Social Media Algorithms

Social media algorithms control what content users see on their feeds and how far it reaches within a network. Understanding how these complex formulas work can help influencers and brands optimize their strategy for maximum visibility. This comprehensive guide delves into cracking the codes of major platforms' algorithms, tailoring content for optimal performance, and employing proven engagement tactics. Read on to unlock the secrets behind social media's black boxes.

Decoding Algorithmic Preferences

Social platforms rely on algorithms to curate the vast amount of content generated by users daily. These complex formulas analyze thousands of signals to determine the "quality" of a post and whether it deserves amplification. While the exact parameters remain closely guarded secrets, research has uncovered some key algorithmic preferences:

Relevancy

Algorithms assess how interesting a post is likely to be for each user based on their profile data, past engagement, and network connections. Content tailored to your target audience has a higher chance of resonating.

Engagement

Posts that generate likes, comments, and shares quickly tell algorithms they are providing value. This signals the content should reach more users, creating a positive feedback loop.

Recency

New, timely content is prioritized to keep feeds fresh and engaging. Older posts progressively lose relevance, although evergreen or frequently reshared content can sometimes break this rule.

Authority

Influential accounts with large, engaged followings are often favored as algorithms assume high-quality content. However, smaller accounts can also gain traction with stellar content.

Video

Video content frequently outperforms images and text in reach as users find it more engaging. Shorter videos under 3 minutes tend to see better completion rates and amplification.

Hashtags

Strategic use of relevant hashtags helps algorithms understand the topic and target users more precisely based on interests. However, excessive hashtag stuffing can backfire.

Captions

Detailed, keyword-optimized captions provide needed context on visual content. Avoid overstuffing hashtags and focus on natural language.

Posting Cadence

Consistently posting valuable content builds authority with algorithms over time. However, overly high frequencies can dilute perceptions of quality.

Negative Signals

Low engagement, spam reports, and account violations all tell algorithms to suppress reach. Avoid engagement bait tactics to build sustainable growth.

While daunting, remembering these core algorithmic preferences can help shape an effective, organic strategy tailored for each platform.

Platform-Specific Strategies

Major social platforms take different approaches to their algorithms, requiring specialized optimization. Here are research-backed tips for the top networks:

Facebook

With over 2 billion monthly active users, Facebook's News Feed algorithm is highly complex. Key strategies include:

- **Prioritize friends and family in content** - Posts that spark connection perform better.
- **Leverage images and video** - Focus on natively uploaded, high-quality visuals.
- **Boost engagement with tags and captions** - Etiquette tagging friends rather than just hashtags.
- **Post consistently 1-2 times daily** - Avoid large gaps or over-saturation.
- **Run regular polls and questions** - Interactive content

drives high levels of engagement.
- **Use Facebook Analytics to identify best post times** - Schedule content when your audience is most active.

Instagram

As a visually driven platform, Instagram's algorithm favors eye-catching content. Tactics include:

- **Post high-quality, natively uploaded photos and videos** - Images should be immersive and authentic.
- **Leverage relevant hashtags in captions and Stories** - Identify niche tags with medium popularity.
- **Engage followers through polls, questions, quizzes** - Instagram Questions is a great interactive feature.
- **Go live regularly** - Live broadcasts are highly promoted by the algorithm.
- **Partner with micro-influencers for organic reach** - Creative collaborations expand your audience.
- **Post consistently 2-3 times daily** - Vary content types from feed posts to Stories.

Twitter

Twitter's real-time feed prioritizes recency, conversations, and engagement signals like retweets. Strategies include:

- **Post timely, trending content** - Use trending hashtags and newsjacking tactics to gain reach.
- **Reply and like frequently** - Join in relevant conversations to increase visibility.

- **Retweet and @ mention influencers** - Strategic connections grow your audience.
- **Ask questions and run polls** - Driving responses ensures engagement.
- **Go live for engagement spikes** - Host talks aligned with your niche.
- **Post 4-5 times daily** - Aim for a balance of original tweets and community interaction.

YouTube

YouTube's algorithm is focused on watch time and viewer satisfaction. Best practices include:

- **Optimize titles, tags, descriptions** - Leverage relevant keywords to help discovery.
- **Implement SEO-friendly practices** - Closed captioning, transcripts, watermarking all boost rank.
- **Promote channel community engagement** - Respond to all comments, run regular polls.
- **Collaborate with synergistic creators** - Cross-promotions introduce new audiences.
- **Analyze audience retention** - Fine-tune video style and structure based on drop-off points.
- **Post 1-2 weekly with consistent schedules** - Enable notifications to maximize viewership of new uploads.
- **Use end screens and cards** - Link to other videos and playlists to boost watch time.

Keeping Up with Algorithm Changes

Social platforms continually refine their algorithms, leaving marketers playing catch up. Here are tips for keeping current:

- **Follow platform announcements and help centers** - Official sources detail upcoming algorithm shifts.
- **Leverage social listening and analytics** - Identify changes through engagement and reach fluctuations.
- **Stay on top of industry news and blogs** - Trusted sites often get insider scoops on updates.
- **Regularly search academic papers and patents** - Technical documents provide algorithm insight.
- **Diversify organic and paid tactics** - Avoid over-reliance on any one channel.
- **Focus on high-quality content and community** - Strong foundations withstand algorithmic turbulence.
- **Remain agile and adaptable** - Be ready to shift strategies to align with algorithmic preferences.

The most effective marketers view algorithms not as obstacles, but opportunities. By decoding platform formulas, they can build sustainable growth strategies that stand the test of time.

SEO for Social Media

Beyond algorithms, old-fashioned search engine optimization (SEO) remains crucial for discovery on social platforms. Tactics include:

Keyword Research

Identify relevant keywords and long-tail variations aligned with your niche using Google Keyword Planner and social listening. Avoid overused terms for focus.

Strong Metadata

Craft compelling titles, descriptions, alt text, and captions using target keywords. This provides signals to both social and search algorithms.

Contextual Links

Use keywords naturally within anchor text when hyperlinking related or external content. This strengthens associations.

Hashtag Optimization

Include a mix of niche and trending hashtags in posts for discoverability while avoiding awkward combinations or overuse.

Localized Content

Tailor posts with location-specific details and hashtags when aiming to reach audiences in particular regions or cities.

Leverage User-Generated Content

Reshare and repost high-quality user photos and videos that incorporate your branded hashtags and handles. This increases visibility.

Profile Optimization

Ensure profile bios and links use critical keywords while keeping the language concise, natural, and compelling.

Social Graph Connections

Growing your social graph by engaging similar accounts and influencers boosts visibility within related networks.

Blending SEO with algorithm-friendly posting establishes a strong foundation for organic reach. Monitor keyword ranks and adjust strategies accordingly.

Timing and Frequency of Posts

When and how often you post shapes content visibility. Follow these best practices tailored to each platform:

Facebook

- Post 1-2 times daily during peak hours from 9 AM to 3 PM and 7 PM to 11 PM.
- Analyze Facebook Insights to identify your audience's most active periods and adjust accordingly.
- Post consistently on weekdays with lighter schedules on weekends when engagement dips.
- Re-share evergreen posts whenever engagement declines to refresh reach.

Instagram

- Post 2-3 times daily, spaced 3-4 hours apart for optimal visibility.
- Post during peak hours between 11 AM to 1 PM on weekdays or Monday evenings.
- Post Stories mid-morning and late afternoon to reach different time zones across geographies.
- Use planning tools to analyze ideal frequencies and schedules based on past performance.

Twitter

- Post 4-5 times daily every 2-3 hours to stay top of mind.
- Leverage Twitter Analytics to find your audience's high traffic periods and align posting schedules.

- Post timely reactions to trending news, events, or holidays for visibility.
- Remember weekends can see high engagement around events or entertainment.

YouTube

- Post 1-2 weekly videos consistently on a fixed schedule viewers can rely on.
- Stick to regular upload days and times to train subscriber notifications.
- Vary content types between long-form, short-form, live streams, and shorts based on audience preferences.
- Use YouTube Analytics to identify low-traffic posting days to avoid and when your subscribers are most active online.

General Tips

- Avoid posting at inconsistent times or with large gaps between posts.
- Use social media management tools to schedule batches of content in advance.
- Always be flexible - monitor performance data and user feedback to adjust frequencies and times as needed.
- Schedule downtime and holidays to avoid burnout.

Finding your optimal posting cadence is a process of continual refinement and experimentation. The ideal frequency and timing balances consistency, value, and quality over quantity.

Using Hashtags and Keywords Effectively

Hashtags and keywords are essential to maximize social media visibility and reach aligned audiences. Best practices include:

Conduct Thorough Research

Use social listening and keyword tools to identify relevant hashtags and keywords aligned with your niche, brand, and campaigns. Look for useful long-tail variations.

Combine Popular and Niche Tags

Include 2-4 highly popular hashtags (#viral, #trending) alongside 4-6 niche community tags for the best visibility. Avoid single-use hashtags.

Localize Content

Use location-based hashtags like city names to engage geo-targeted audiences. Identify localized keywords.

Create Unique Branded Tags

Launch custom hashtags for special campaigns, promotions, or events. Encourage user-generated content integration.

Use Hashtags in Stories

Leverage sticker, quiz, polls, question, and slider features in Stories to integrate hashtags. This broadens reach.

Avoid Forced Combinations

While some platforms like long hashtag strings, combinations should flow naturally. Don't force irrelevant tags just for visibility.

Monitor Performance

Analyze hashtag and keyword metrics through platform analytics to identify top performers to reuse and low-performers to eliminate.

Refresh Frequently

Continually research new niche tags and keywords to stay aligned with trends and community discussions.

Hashtags distill complex ideas into discoverable symbols. When used strategically, they become powerful tools for reaching aligned audiences.

Encouraging User Interaction

Driving high engagement dramatically improves content reach and positioning with algorithms. Tactics for fueling participation include:

Ask Questions

Pose timely questions and polls aligned with your niche to spark discussion in captions and comments. Respond to all answers.

Run Contests and Challenges

Creative user-generated content challenges expand brand awareness while stocking future content. Offer prizes to incentivize entries.

Curate User Content

Repost great user photos or videos leveraging your branded hashtags with permission and proper credits. This recognizes community members.

Go Live Frequently

Broadcast live talks, Q&As, behind-the-scenes footage, or virtual events to enable two-way engagement.

Leverage Interactive Tools

Use built-in stickers, quizzes, questions, and other interactive features to drive comments and shares.

Share "Behind the Scenes"

Provide exclusive, "inside access" style content to show authenticity and strengthen connections with followers.

Spark Debate

Post opinions, reviews, or comparisons that invite friendly debates based on niche interests and passions.

Respond to All Comments

Reply promptly to all user comments with thoughtful answers and appreciation for their time and insights.

Remember, social media is meant for conversations, not broadcasts. The more you interact, the more the algorithms will amplify your presence.

Creating Shareable Content

While quality original content is the foundation, shaping posts for maximum sharing potential can dramatically expand reach. Tactics include:

Leverage Trends and Newsjack

Create content that taps into what is currently popular or experiencing a viral moment to ride algorithmic waves.

Appeal to Emotions

Craft content focused on inspiring hope, joy, laughter, wonder, nostalgia - positive emotions proven to boost engagement.

Target Interest-Based Communities

Tailor posts with niche pop culture references, insider language, and topics specific communities are passionate about.

Offer Exclusive Value

Promote giveaways, discounts, first-looks, or exclusive resources only available to your followers as a sharing incentive.

Collaborate with Nano-Influencers

Partner with niche micro-influencers (under 10k followers) to tap into their engaged communities with co-created content.

Leverage UGC Contests

Challenge users to create branded content and reshare their entries. Feature standouts on your channels.

Include Strong Calls-to-Action

Prompt next steps like tagging friends, checking links, or using specific hashtags to drive shares.

Analyze Shareability Factors

Review past top performing posts to identify common themes, formats, headlines, or content types that resonate for replication.

Shareability is a skill that improves over time through experience, creativity, and diligent optimization based on performance data. Keep testing what makes your audience hit that share button.

Hosting Live Sessions and Q&As

Both Facebook and Instagram emphasize live video, boosting broadcast reach substantially. Best practices for success include:

Promote in Advance

Build buzz by sharing scheduled broadcast times, special guests, and tempting previews on your other social channels.

Stream Guest Experts or Influencers

Invite niche personalities like authors or athletes for "virtual sit downs" aligned with your audience's interests.

Incorporate Audience Q&As

Dedicate portions of the live session to answer follower-submitted questions to recognize them.

Choose Compelling Locations

For IRL streams, select visually interesting settings like conferences, events, or relevant geographic locales.

Promote Channel Content

Discuss new videos, upcoming releases, contests, or platform features to direct viewers to high-value content.

Maintain Engagement

Keep the conversation lively by asking questions, running quick polls and challenges, and reacting to comments in real-time.

Save and Repurpose Content

Download streams to reuse excerpts as shorts or compilations. Transcribe for podcasts.

The organic reach and follower engagement driven by live social content make it a highly valuable but underutilized tactic for influencer marketing.

Final Thoughts on Mastering Social Media Algorithms

While social platforms love touting the "meaningful connections" algorithms foster, they rarely reveal just how those formulas work. However, savvy influencers willing to move beyond the hype and analyze the data can decipher the codes powering visibility. This guides creation of high-performing, algorithm-optimized content strategies tailored for each platform.

The keys are understanding core algorithmic preferences, continually optimizing based on analytics, and exploring proven engagement-driving tactics. With the right balance of art and science, you can master the social media black boxes to take your reach to new heights.

Remember, algorithms will keep evolving. Flexibility and diligent tuning are essential. But the foundations of valuable, quality content and authentic community connections will ultimately win the social media game long-term.

FAQs About Mastering Social Media Algorithms

What are the most important factors in social media algorithms?

The top algorithmic ranking signals are engagement (likes, comments, shares), content quality, account authority, relevancy to audience interests, recency, video format, and strategic use of captions, tags, and keywords.

How often should I post on social media to beat the algorithms?

Ideal posting frequency varies by platform, but 1-3 daily posts for Facebook, 2-4 for Twitter, 2-3 for Instagram, and 1-2 weekly for YouTube are good starting points before customizing further.

What types of content do best with social media algorithms?

Video and image content tend to outperform text, interactive posts and Stories drive high engagement, while newsjacking trends and leveraging UGC also attract algorithm promotion.

How do I find the best hashtags and keywords for social media?

Conduct keyword research using social listening tools and look for relevant niche hashtags trending among your target community. Identify customized branded hashtags and keywords to boost discovery.

Should I use a social media scheduler or post manually?

Social media management platforms that allow batch scheduling and analytics integration are extremely helpful productivity tools. But also ensure some real-time manual interaction.

15

Building a Loyal Pet Influencer Community

A dedicated, engaged community is the lifeblood of any successful social media influencer. While stunning photos and clever captions may attract an initial wave of followers, cultivating an authentic connection and sense of belonging with your audience is what transforms casual fans into loyal brand advocates.

For pet influencers especially, the pressure to build not just a following, but a **community**, is paramount. People don't just want cute animal photos - they want to feel like part of your pet's world.

In this chapter, we'll explore proven strategies to foster an engaged, supportive pet influencer community that sticks with you over the long-haul.

Fostering a Dedicated Audience

Building a loyal community starts with understanding your followers and creating content that resonates with them. But it requires more than just posting great photos. You need to actively engage your audience and encourage two-way communication.

Encouraging Regular Engagement

Posting incredible pet photos will naturally get people's attention. But to convert followers into true fans, you need them to move beyond passive consumption and actively participate.

Some ways to encourage engagement include:

- **Asking questions:** Pose questions in captions related to the photo or your pet. This could be asking for caption ideas, opinions on products/topics, or just creating a fun polls.
- **Responding to comments:** Don't just post and run! Reply to as many comments as you can, especially in the first few hours after posting. This shows followers you value their contributions.
- **Sharing user generated content:** Repost great photos, videos, art or stories that followers have tagged or sent you. This validates them as co-creators.
- **Using Instagram Lives:** Broadcast behind-the-scenes footage with your pet. Followers love the raw, unedited peek into your pet's everyday adventures.
- **Leveraging Instagram Stories:** Use interactive stickers

in Stories like Q&As, polls and quizzes to spark two-way engagement.

The more you interact directly with followers, the more invested they will become in you and your pet's journey.

Building a Sense of Community

Beyond just engaging, you want to cultivate a feeling of community among your followers. People are drawn to not just your pet, but the relationships and friendships that form around your account.

Some ways to build community include:

- Giving your followers a **nickname**. This creates an identity and group affiliation. For example, fans of famous French Bulldog Jiff Pom are "Jiffstronauts".
- Creating **user generated content campaigns**. For example, ask followers to post photos of their pets in funny hats. This bandwagon effect generates a flood of community participation.
- Organizing collaborative **group projects**. For example, ask each person to submit a 1-second video with their pet. Then edit them together into a long video showcasing all your fans.
- Hosting **giveaways** for your most active, loyal supporters. Offering prizes, custom merchandise or shoutouts rewards your VIP followers.
- Sending exclusive content to **email subscribers**. For example, blooper reels, behind-the-scenes footage or candid photos build a sense of exclusivity.

- Planning **in-person events** like meetups, parties or group outings that bring your online community into the real world.

Fostering a spirit of camaraderie and inclusion among supporters transforms your personal brand into a thriving, engaged community.

Providing Value to Followers

While fun and entertainment keep people initially interested, followers will only stay loyal if you also provide value. Consider what benefits you offer that truly improve your audience's lives.

Some ways pet influencers provide value include:

- **Behind-the-scenes access** - Letting fans into your pet's daily life makes them feel special.
- **Pet care education** - Share training and health tips that followers can apply to their own pets.
- **Product reviews** - Provide useful reviews on pet items so owners make informed buying choices.
- **Pet parenting advice** - Offer troubleshooting tips on common issues like leash pulling, barking, anxiety etc.
- **Pet entertainment** - Supply an endless stream of delightful, stress-relieving animal content.
- **Pet inspiration** - Motivate people to adopt rescue animals and be the best pet parents.
- **Sense of community** - Fulfill the human need for connection through a shared love of animals.
- **Access to brands/sponsors** - Partner with companies

your audience loves to bring them exclusive deals and products.

Delivering genuine value earns loyal advocates who become deeply invested in your ongoing success.

Community Management Strategies

Once you've built an initial audience of fans, you need to actively manage your community to keep it healthy and engaged. Setting boundaries and moderating effectively transforms random followers into a harmonious ecosystem.

Responding to Comments and Messages

Pet influencers often get inundated with comments and DMs. While it's impossible to respond to everything, you should aim to maintain an active, visible presence in replying.
Some tips for community management include:

- **Set expectations** - Let your audience know when you're most reachable, and when not to expect a reply. For example, "I respond to all messages between 3-5pm daily".
- **Create FAQs** - Compose an Instagram highlight or Story addressing your most common questions and comments. This reduces repetitive inquiries.
- **Respond visibly** - When you do reply, respond directly on the post/photo itself rather than buried in DMs. This shows all followers you're engaged.
- **Delegate help** - Enlist a social media manager, family

member or friend to help field a portion of messages and questions.

- **Use tools** - Services like Hootsuite can help manage, filter and respond to messages in bulk.

Frequent, consistent interaction, even in small touches, makes followers feel heard and appreciated.

Managing Online Communities

As communities grow large, you'll need to set ground rules and guidelines for civil participation. Some options include:

- **Community policies** - Create rules addressing topics like harassment, advertising, political talk etc. and consequences for violations.
- **Automated filters** - Use keywords and tools to auto-block offensive language, spam links etc.
- **Banned words** - Prevent certain divisive terms commonly abused by trolls.
- **Block liberally** - Don't hesitate to block abusive users. Protect your peace of mind and community.
- **Designate moderators** - Appoint trustworthy followers as voluntary moderators to report issues.
- **Limit DMs** - Disable open DMs if you're being harassed or overwhelmed via private messages.

Healthy communities require reasonable guardrails. Set standards aligned with your values.

Handling Negative Feedback

No matter how sunny of a personality you have, negativity will inevitably rear its head in any social space. Handling criticism with grace prevents isolated issues from rippling into community turmoil.

Some tips include:

- **Respond calmly** - If you lose your cool, it often escalates issues rather than defusing them.
- **Acknowledge politely** - A simple "Thank you for the feedback, I appreciate you taking the time to share this." can neutralize many critics.
- **Move the conversation** - Redirect to a positive topic related to their comment rather than debating.
- **Block if necessary** - You have no obligation to accept abuse or harassment. Unfollow or restrict aggressive accounts.
- **Turn mistakes into lessons** - If the feedback has validity, own it sincerely and share how you'll improve.
- **Listen more** - Negative feedback, while uncomfortable, often surfaces issues worth paying attention to. Keep an open mind.

Channeling negativity into opportunities for growth and dialogue demonstrates responsive, responsible community leadership.

Creating Community-Centric Events

In addition to day-to-day management, pet influencers can spur huge engagement spikes by organizing special community events. These create anticipation, foster deeper bonds with followers, and keep your account dynamic.

Hosting Online Events and Contests

Interactive online events turn passive followers into enthusiastic participants. Some popular options include:

- **Caption contests** - Post a photo and have followers compete to write the funniest, cleverest caption.
- **Giveaways** - Partner with a pet brand to offer prizes, merch or free products to select fans.
- **Hashtag campaigns** - Invite fans to post their own pet photos around a dedicated hashtag like #TongueOutTuesday.
- **IG Lives** - Broadcast real-time videos of activities with your pet like park visits, training sessions or playtime.
- **Takeovers** - Let fans voluntarily "take over" your IG Story for a day to give their pet's POV.
- **Pet parenting Q&As** - Go Live and take questions from viewers about pet care advice.
- **Pet trivia** - Host a live game show testing fans' knowledge of your pet's history, quirks and claims-to-fame.

Online events allow widespread community participation and reward dedication with prizes, clout and exclusive access.

Organizing Meet-ups and Gatherings

For pet influencers able to meet followers in-person, hosting real world gatherings can take community connection to the next level. Some ideas include:

- **Pet-friendly venues** - Hold meet-ups at dog parks, pet stores or animal shelters so fans can bring their pets.
- **Pet expos** - Rent vendor space at a local expo and promote a dedicated meet-up time.
- **Photo opps** - Offer at a specified time and place for fans to get professional photos taken with you and your pet.
- **Pet parties** - Host an online RSVP party at your home or yard for local followers and their pets to socialize. Consider pet-friendly refreshments.
- **Pet charity events** - Organize a community gathering tied to fundraising, donations drives, or volunteering for a local animal welfare non-profit.

While online communities are powerful, face-to-face events offer your biggest fans the ultimate engagement - a chance to meet the famous pet and influencer in the fur and flesh!

Collaborative Projects with the Community

Tap into your followers' talents and creativity by organizing collaborative community projects. For example:

- **Crowdsourced merchandise** - Invite fans to submit designs to be voted on and produced into limited-edition community merch.

- **Pet yearbook** - Have supporters send in photos and captions highlighting their favorite memories with your pet over the years. Compile into a digital yearbook.
- **Tagged pet art** - Encourage artistic followers to create original fanart and tag you to be reshared.
- **Pet profiles** - Ask fans to post short profiles introducing their pets. Repost a rotating featured #PetOfTheWeek.
- **Fan spotlights** - Highlight notable supporters by featuring their accounts, pets and talents.
- **Community newsletter** - Recruit volunteer contributors to help assemble articles, spotlights, and features about your pet influencer community.

Collaborative projects allow fans to leave their creative pawprint on your account and deepen their sense of ownership in your pet's brand.

Final Thoughts: Building a Loyal Pet Influencer Community

While amassing followers is an impressive feat, cultivating an engaged community is the more valuable and rewarding endeavor for pet influencers. Allow time for authentic connections to flourish. Invest in responding thoughtfully and adding value. And don't hesitate to block trolls, limit overwhelm, and set boundaries to maintain your peace-of-mind.

Most importantly, remember that the community you build is not just a stepping stone on your influencer journey - it's the destination. Treasure it and continue putting in the work to nurture those relationships long after follower counts plateau.

Stay committed to fostering a supportive, collaborative environment and your community will stick with you through thick, thin, and anything this wild ride of pet influencer fame throws your way.

FAQs: Building a Loyal Pet Influencer Community

What are some tips to build a loyal pet influencer community?

Some top tips include:

- Encourage 2-way engagement through questions, polls, sharing user generated content and replying to comments.
- Build community spirit through inclusive language (like calling fans a nickname), collaborative projects and exclusive access.
- Provide true value to followers through education, entertainment, pet care advice and access to brands.
- Set community guidelines and moderate effectively to maintain a positive environment.
- Respond visibly to negative feedback calmly and constructively.
- Create special events and contests to generate excitement and participation.
- Organize in-real-life meetups when possible to connect offline.
- Involve your audience creatively through crowdsourced content and community partnerships.

How much time should pet influencers spend engaging with their audience each day?

It's recommended to spend 30-60 minutes minimum per day actively engaging with your audience. Set a consistent time you can dedicate to:

- Responding to comments, especially in the first 1-3 hours after posting.
- Replying to Instagram DMs and comments.
- Reviewing and sharing user generated content.
- Liking and commenting on followers' posts.
- Planning your engagement and content calendar.

Consider also scheduling 1-2 days a week for deeper community care like:

- Responding in-depth to messages.
- Providing thoughtful feedback and advice to followers.
- Creating content highlighting fans.
- Handling account appeals from blocked followers.
- Identifying harassment/negativity and moderating.

What types of content best engage pet influencer followers?

The most engaging content taps into the human need for connection. Followers love:

- Funny or cute captions showing your pet's personality.
- Close-up shots highlighting unique details about your pet.

- Blooper reels and behind-the-scenes looks at the chaos behind poised pictures.
- Videos of your pet playing, hanging out or going on adventures.
- User generated content from fans.
- Interactive polls, questions, memes and hashtag campaigns.
- Responding to commenters and featuring fan content.
- Celebrating your most loyal supporters.
- Live, in-the-moment updates through Instagram Lives or Stories.
- Holiday and event-themed posts fans can relate to.

How can pet influencers handle negativity and trolls while maintaining a positive community?

It's important to set expectations for civil participation. Some tips:

- Disable open DMs if you're being harassed privately.
- Create automated filters to block offensive language.
- Designate volunteer moderators to report abuse.
- Block users at the first sign of harassment - don't tolerate it.
- Limit political talk and other divisive topics.
- Respond calmly and acknowledge feedback without debating trolls.
- Share community guidelines detailing what's not tolerated.
- Redirect the conversation to positivity.
- Turn mistakes into lessons if valid issues are raised.

- Monitor closely after publicity spikes for influxes of negativity.

The healthiest communities balance openness with protective boundaries. Never be afraid to block those who detract from the supportive environment you're building.

What are some fun contests/events for pet influencers to engage their audience?

Some fun community event ideas include:

- Caption contests on a cute or funny pet photo.
- Regular hashtag days like #TongueOutTuesday or #FurryFriday.
- Giveaways partnering with a pet brand to offer prizes.
- Pet trivia live on Instagram to test fans' knowledge.
- Polls asking for followers' opinions on products, pet topics or account ideas.
- Takeovers featuring fan pets "hosting" your Instagram Story.
- Pet talent shows inviting fans to submit videos of tricks and skills.
- Designing merch collaboratively by crowdsourcing ideas.
- Photo contests awarding prizes for images with your branded hashtag.
- Scavenger hunts sending followers on adventures to unlock rewards.
- Pet birthday parties with themed decorations and games.

Keep it novel, interactive, and focused on celebrating your

engaged supporters!

16

Overcoming Challenges in Pet Influencing

Becoming a successful pet influencer takes passion, persistence, and creativity. However, even the most dedicated petfluencers inevitably face obstacles on their journey to growth and longevity in this dynamic industry. This chapter explores common challenges pet influencers encounter, along with actionable strategies for overcoming plateaus, avoiding burnout, mitigating copycats, and ultimately, continuing to thrive despite hurdles along the way.

Dealing with Plateaus and Setbacks

A "plateau" occurs when a pet influencer's growth stagnates. This may show up as a dip in engagement, slowing follower count, or gradual decline in revenue. While disheartening, plateaus are a normal part of any social media journey. By identifying causes and responding appropriately, petfluencers can regain momentum.

Identifying Causes of Growth Stagnation

Pinpointing the root of stagnation is key to mapping an effective solution. Common causes include:

- **Content fatigue:** Posting repetitive content without innovation. Followers lose interest in more of the same.
- **Algorithm changes:** Platform algorithm updates that impact visibility. Staying atop each network's algorithm is an ongoing challenge.
- **Increased competition:** With more pet influencers arises more competitive noise. Consistency and uniqueness are key to cutting through.
- **Life changes:** Major life events like moves, pregnancies/babies, or demanding jobs can reduce content output and social media focus. Readjusting is required to balance priorities.
- **Burnout:** Pet influencing as a full-time gig can be draining. Burnout leads to less enthusiasm and creativity in content.
- **Pandemic shifts:** COVID-19 has impacted partnerships and campaigns. Travel restrictions also limit content opportunities. Adapting is critical.

Assessing what may be impacting your growth helps determine the best path forward. Be honest about any areas you've slipped up in or ways life has thrown your business a curveball. There's no shame in churn—just opportunity for improvement.

Strategies for Overcoming Obstacles

Armed with knowledge of what's hindering your growth, here are proactive tips to drive momentum:

- **Switch up content:** Try new content formats, topics, and angles. Surprise followers with fresh, unexpected content. Doing the same old thing leads to plateau.
- **Improve SEO:** Research top keywords and optimize titles, captions, hashtags, and transcripts. Improving discoverability helps counter algorithm changes.
- **Collaborate:** Partner with fellow petfluencers for cross-promotions, shoutouts, and co-created content. Strategic collaborations expand your reach.
- **Interact consistently:** Reply to comments, engage with industry peers, and post Stories regularly. Being present nurtures community.
- **Analyze performance:** Utilize each platform's analytics to see what content resonates best. Double down on what's working.
- **Post more frequently:** Increase output without compromising quality. The more content you create, the more chances for engagement.
- **Explore emerging platforms:** Diversify by establishing a presence on up-and-coming networks like Lomotif, Likee, or Twitch.
- **Attend events:** Connect in-person at conferences and conventions post-pandemic. Networking helps forge partnerships.
- **Revisit your niche:** Ensure your pet's niche still aligns with your passions. Tweaking your niche can reinvigorate

content.

- **Take a break:** Sometimes the best solution is stepping back. A short content hiatus with social media limits can provide clarity. Come back renewed.

While stagnation feels discouraging, it's usually temporary with the right strategies. Be patient, get creative, and keep loving what you do. Consistency pays off in the long run.

Staying Motivated During Tough Times

When slogging through a plateau, morale may take a hit. Here are ways to stay motivated:

- **Track progress:** Look back on growth achieved already—proof your influence is increasing overall, even if presently stalled.
- **Set micro-goals:** Focus on daily or weekly mini objectives like content output rather than big-picture goals. Small progress fuels motivation.
- **Find inspiration:** Look to fellow petfluencers who over-came slumps. Their perseverance can re-energize you.
- **Focus on enjoyment:** Remind yourself why you enjoy creating pet content, separate from any success metrics. Creating content you love is sustainable motivation.
- **Connect with community:** The support of fellow pet lovers and petfluencers provides strength during down periods. You're not alone.
- **Reward milestones:** Celebrate wins like follower increases or campaign achievements. Acknowledge progress through lows.

- **Take breaks:** Stepping back to recharge is perfectly acceptable. You can't pour from an empty cup. Come back rejuvenated.
- **Get accountable:** Share your goals and journey with someone supportive who will keep you motivated and honest. Accountability fosters results.
- **Be your own cheerleader:** Hype up your accomplishments on tough days. Confidence and celebrating wins, big or small, boosts morale.

Persistence through lows bears fruit. Staying motivated sets you up for success when growth kicks back into gear.

Navigating Content Burnout

Burnout is a formidable obstacle for full-time petfluencers. Demand for frequent, high-quality content is draining. Without intervention, burnout torpedo's motivation and creativity. Implement these strategies to avoid and overcome burnout.

Recognizing Signs of Burnout

Watch for these indicators that burnout is setting in:

- Dreading creating content
- Decreased engagement and growth
- Loss of creativity; repetitive content
- Feeling frustrated, defeated or overwhelmed
- Lack of enjoyment or passion for your work
- Fatigue, headaches or irritability
- Poor sleep, changes in appetite

- Difficulty concentrating
- Increased mistakes
- Feeling isolated and withdrawn

Any combination of these symptoms over an extended period indicates impending burnout. The sooner you recognize the signs, the quicker you can take action.

Tips for Refreshing Content

Staving off burnout means staying excited about content creation. Try these tips:

Repurpose evergreen content: Give old content new life by resharing or repackaging into different formats like blogs, reels or videos. Adding a new spin reengages followers.

** Experiment with formats:** Challenge yourself to attempt new styles like vlogs, stop motion, boomerangs or sketches. Creativity thrives on variety.

Feature fan content: Sharing user-generated content like #pet ircus submissions or reviews provides a break while engaging your audience.

Go behind the scenes: Give followers a peek behind the petfluencing curtain with content about your processes, gear, or business milestones. show the person behind the pet.

Spotlight employees: Involve your team members in content with Q&As, takeovers or spotlights on photographers, designers, etc. This provides fresh perspectives.

Get interactive: Polls, AMAs, challenges and contests allow audiences to actively participate in content. Two-way engagement boosts morale.

Trying new approaches keeps your content—and you—

charged up. Followers appreciate variety as well. Keep exploring formats, topics and angles.

Balancing Creativity and Wellness

Avoiding burnout ultimately comes down to work-life balance. It's easy for petfluencing to consume your whole life. Prioritize self-care with these principles:

- **Unplug regularly.** Set limits on working hours and designate tech-free times. Disconnecting allows you to recharge.
- **Take time off.** Use vacations and staycations to completely disengage. You deserve breaks to nurture your wellbeing.
- **Set boundaries.** Be clear on work hours, availability and project timelines. Sticking to boundaries prevents burnout.
- **Prioritize sleep.** Adequate sleep is crucial for mental health. Follow sleep hygiene principles and guard your bedtime.
- **Move your body.** Make time for exercise, hiking, sports or other physical activities. Movement reduces stress.
- **Eat nutritious foods.** Fuel your body with whole foods. Avoid using unhealthy eating as a coping mechanism.
- **Pursue hobbies.** Allot time for leisure activities beyond petfluencing. Art, reading, games—do what enriches you.
- **Connect with loved ones.** Relationships outside work add valuable perspective. Make bonding with friends and family a priority.
- **Seek support.** Don't isolate yourself if burnout hits.

Confide in trusted friends or a therapist. Talk it out.

- **Say no.** Avoid overcommitting. Learn to decline requests that overwhelm you. Give yourself permission to set limits.

Your mental and physical wellbeing enables creativity long-term. Keep yourself—not just your content—renewed.

Handling Competition and Copycats

As the petfluencing industry grows more saturated, you'll inevitably encounter increased competition and content mimickers. Navigating these situations gracefully and professionally is key.

Differentiating Your Pet's Brand

The best defense against copycats is establishing a distinctive brand. Consider these differentiation strategies:

- **Highlight your pet's personality.** Let your pet's quirks shine through in content. Authenticity is hard to copy.
- **Lean into your niche.** Own a specific niche like adventure pets or senior pets. Become known as the authority in your specialty.
- **Develop signature content.** Create reoccurring content types, hashtag campaigns or series unique to you. Consistency builds association.
- **Collaborate across niches.** Partner with petfluencers in unrelated niches to expose each other's audiences to new types of content.

184

- **Utilize high-quality photography/videography.** Invest in pro equipment and collaborators to make your content production value exceed competitors.
- **Focus on storytelling.** Weave your pet's tale throughout content to build audience connection. Storytelling keeps fans invested in you long-term.
- **Be real about challenges.** Being vulnerable sharing the struggles on your petfluencing journey resonates. Rawness earns trust.

Leaning into originality makes your content less replicable. Your pet has character all their own—flaunt it.

Healthy Competition vs. Copying

Imitation may be flattery, but plaigarism and riding coattails is unethical. Set yourself apart with integrity:

- **Innovate, don't imitate.** Be inspired by others, but develop your own signature style. Copying others' content verbatim is never okay.
- **Credit inspiration.** If drawing ideas from another creator, mention how their work sparked your concept. Give credit where it's due.
- **Add value.** Don't just piggyback trends—provide a novel spin. Followers want to see your unique take on a concept.
- **Inform copycats kindly.** If someone rips off your content, politely inform them. Assume good intent. They may not realize their misstep.
- **Report only if necessary.** As a last resort, report extreme cases of content theft to platforms. Always try open

communication first.

- **View competitors as collaborators.** Having peers elevates the industry overall. Find ways to team up vs. tear down.

Focus less on what others do, and more on nurturing your own creativity. Originality wins long-term.

Protecting Your Intellectual Property

You have full rights to monetize and protect the content you create. Take these proactive measures:

- **Trademark your brand.** Register your pet's brand name and logo with the USPTO to gain exclusive commercial rights.
- **Register copyrights.** Submit copyright forms to the US Copyright Office for names, slogan, videos and images. This proves legal ownership.
- **Add watermarks.** Visibly watermark images and videos to deter theft. Only provide unmarked files to paid clients.
- **Draft contracts.** Create partnership contracts requiring consent for use of your content. Outline usage terms, compensation and ownership rights.
- **Leverage DMCA.** Report copyright violations under the Digital Millennium Copyright Act via takedown notices. This can result in legal action if infringements persist.
- **Consult an attorney.** Consider having an intellectual property attorney review your documents and provide tailored legal advice as needed. Their counsel fortifies your protections.

While rarely needed, having the proper legal protections empowers you to defend your work. Focus first on creating stellar content only you can make.

Final Thoughts: Overcoming Petfluencing Challenges

Like any worthwhile endeavor, petfluencing comes with growing pains. From plateaus to competition, challenges arise at all levels of success. However, with savvy strategies these hurdles are surmountable. Authenticity, ingenuity and balance provide the stamina needed for the long game. Your passion keeps propelling you forward.

Stay nimble and proactive in the face of obstacles. The reward of doing what you love—with your beloved pet by your side—is worth weathering any storm. Keep your "why" at the forefront, and you will continue to influence in good times and bad. Your unique voice and vision matter—never doubt that. With smart planning and self-care, your petfluencing path can avoid pitfalls and scale new heights. Now go unleash your potential.

FAQs: Overcoming Petfluencing Challenges

What causes growth plateaus for pet influencers?

Most growth plateaus result from content fatigue, algorithm changes, increased competition, life changes, burnout, pandemic shifts, or some combination of these factors. Pinpointing the root cause is key to getting back on track.

How can pet influencers stay motivated during tough times?

Useful motivation tips include tracking progress made, setting micro-goals, finding inspiration from others, focusing on enjoyment, connecting with community, rewarding milestones, taking breaks, getting accountable, and self-cheerleading.

What are some early signs pet influencers may experience burnout?

Look out for dread toward creating content, decreased engagement, repetitive content, frustration/defeat/overwhelm, lack of enjoyment, fatigue/irritability, poor sleep and appetite changes, difficulty concentrating, isolation, and frequent mistakes. Addressing burnout promptly minimizes its damage.

What strategies help pet influencers create fresh, engaging content?

Repurposing evergreen content, experimenting with new formats, featuring fan content, going behind the scenes, spotlighting team members, getting interactive, and analyzing metrics can all provide inspiration for keeping content creative.

How should pet influencers respond to copycats and content competitors?

Focus on innovating vs. imitating, give credit to those who inspire you, add value to trends you participate in, kindly inform copycats of misuse, report only if essential, view competitors as collaborators, and protect your IP. Taking the high road preserves your reputation.

17

The Ethics of Pet Influencing

Pet influencing has exploded in popularity over the last decade. As more pet owners gain massive followings by showcasing their furry friends online, the industry surrounding pet fame has ballooned. But with great popularity comes great responsibility. For pet influencers, ethical considerations around animal welfare, authenticity, transparency, and social impact have become increasingly important. This chapter explores the key ethical issues arising in pet influencing today, and how influencers can navigate them with care.

Ensuring Pet Welfare and Happiness

At its core, pet influencing revolves around showcasing adorable, photogenic animals for an enraptured online audience. But maintaining a pet's welfare and happiness should always be the top priority for influencers. Several ethical factors come into play.

Prioritizing Pet Health and Comfort

First and foremost, pet influencers must ensure the basic health and comfort of their animals at all times. This means providing appropriate food, enrichment activities, veterinary care, grooming, and safe spaces for rest. Pets should never be put in dangerous or frightening situations just for the sake of a photoshot or video.

Signs of stress, anxiety, or fear exhibited by pets during content creation are major red flags. Pets may pant, pace, whine, lick their lips, or show other body language indicating discomfort. Being attuned to these signals and stopping any activity that evokes them is essential. Rushing through a photoshoot while ignoring a pet's obvious anxiety is unethical.

Pet influencers should also avoid promoting participation in activities that could pose health risks or injuries to pets simply for entertainment value. These include eating unsuitable human foods, wearing restrictive costumes, or performing unnatural tricks.

Overall, the pet's needs must take clear precedence over content creation. Their comfort and safety should never be compromised.

Ethical Considerations in Content Creation

Influencers walk a fine line during photoshoots and video production. While entertaining content is the goal, they must consider whether certain scenarios are in the pet's best interests.

For example, placing pets in cluttered spaces, precarious positions, or close proximity with props or costumes carries risks. Pets could become stressed, anxious, injured, or even choke on small pieces. Careful setup of engaging but safe scenes is paramount.

The use of artificial lights, camera flashes, noisy equipment, and bustling crews can also impact pet welfare. Ensuring proper acclimation and limiting stressful stimulus is key. If a pet exhibits signs of fear or anxiety, filming should cease immediately.

Short filming sessions with ample breaks, praise, treats, and a chance to decompress are ideal for the animal's well-being. Rushing through long, uninterrupted shoots ignores a pet's fundamental need for rest. Their health should never be sacrificed for more content.

Balancing Fame and Well-Being

As a pet's online popularity grows, managing the influx of opportunities becomes crucial. Their fame can quickly scale beyond a healthy balance if not kept in check.

The lure of wealth and notoriety could lead influencers to accept too many brand sponsorships, appearances, travel demands, public events, and content requests. But preserving a pet's routine, minimizing stress, and avoiding overstimulation should take precedence.

Setting clear boundaries around the pet's involvement, refusing overwhelming demands, and giving them space from the spotlight is essential. Their well-being must not be compromised by the desire for ever-more money and followers.

With careful limits in place, pets can comfortably enjoy the positives of fame like playtime, treats and quality time spent with their beloved owners. But influencers have an ethical duty not to exploit their pet's popularity for personal gain. Their health and happiness should remain the top concern.

Authentic Representation and Honesty

Authenticity and honesty are fundamental for pet influencers hoping to build trust and community. Misrepresenting pets through tactics like forced posing, fake captions or misleading editing erodes follower relationships. Upholding transparency should be a top priority.

Transparency with Followers

Showing pets in natural states is important, not misrepresenting their personalities. For example, an influencer shouldn't claim their pet "loves wearing costumes and posing for photos" when they clearly dislike it. Being transparent about a pet's actual temperament builds trust.

Likewise, acknowledging when pets misbehave rather than covering it up conveys authenticity. Followers will relate to the genuine personality and quirks of a pet, flaws and all. They want unfiltered truth, not a fabricated illusion of perfection.

Caption transparency is also key. Influencers shouldn't invent fictional backstories or sensationalize normal pet behaviors for engagement. Exaggerated captions damage credibility over time.

Honesty also applies to disclosure when posts involve paid sponsorships. FTC guidelines require influencers to clearly indicate branded content so as not to mislead followers. Ethical influencers abide by these regulations diligently.

Avoiding Misleading or False Information

Post captions should provide useful, accurate information on pet care and welfare, not spread misleading claims or falsehoods. Followers look to influencers as trusted sources of knowledge.

This means thoroughly researching any health, diet, training or other pet-related advice given to the audience. Citing credible sources and experts is ideal. If proper research hasn't been done, it's best not to offer specific guidance.

Influencers also shouldn't make exaggerated or outright false claims about sponsor products. This includes asserting health benefits, performance capabilities or other attributes without independent verification. Followers expect total honesty in recommendations.

Presenting facts in proper context is also important. Data, statistics or scientific research should never be twisted to fit a desired narrative. Audiences appreciate influencers who remain committed to full transparency.

Ethical Brand Collaborations

As digital stars, pet influencers get bombarded with sponsorship opportunities. But not all brand partnerships align with their ethics.

Promoting products with dubious quality claims or possible health risks to pets is irresponsible. Followers notice when recommendations seem financially motivated rather than in the pet's best interests. Partnering only with brands they actually use and genuinely believe in is key.

Influencers should also avoid sponsorships for pet products that encourage irresponsible ownership. This includes impulse pet purchases, normalization of dangerous breeds, or painting exotic pets as mainstream pets. Such brands often misrepresent complex ethical issues.

Sponsorships with ethics-focused companies committed to pet health and welfare are ideal. Followers pay attention to where influencers direct their publicity, so these alignments matter.

By carefully vetting potential partners, pet influencers can leverage their fame for positive change and maintain their integrity. Their sponsorships should reflect their true values.

Sustainable and Responsible Influencing

With great followings comes great responsibility beyond just pets themselves. Pet influencers now consider their broader social impact as prominent voices in the online space. This encompasses environmental consciousness, philanthropic causes and promoting animal welfare.

Environmental Considerations

The meteoric rise of pet influencing has certainly contributed to culture's heavy digital footprint. From energy-guzzling photo shoots to pet products shipped worldwide, influencers must now consider how their activities affect the planet.

Several climate-conscious practices help, like:

· Minimizing air travel for appearances/events
· Supporting eco-friendly brands
· Using energy efficient lighting and gear

- Choosing reusable rather than disposable props
- Recycling content costumes and accessories

Donating to or partnering with environmental groups also shows commitment to sustainability. More broadly, pet influencers have a chance to raise awareness on ecological issues for the betterment of all creatures, great and small.

Supporting Animal Welfare Causes

Lending their powerful platforms to support animal welfare nonprofits makes an enormous difference. Sharing rescue stories attracts donor/adopter attention and mobilizes followers into action for good.

Influencers can spotlight organizations providing low-cost veterinary services, community care, rehoming services, disaster relief, wildlife conservation, anti-cruelty efforts and more. Their reach offers a megaphone for this advocacy work.

They may also coordinate social media fundraisers, promote donation campaigns, foster/adopt rescues themselves and encourage political engagement on animal issues. Converting pet fame into tangible impact upholds ethical values.

Promoting Positive Social Impact

Pet influencers act as role models for millions of adoring fans. They now recognize how their content shapes attitudes/behavior around animals and human responsibility. Promoting informed, ethical pet ownership is a crucial opportunity.

This means using their platforms to advocate for:

- Adopting over buying pets
- Spaying/neutering to reduce overpopulation
- Vet care, training, proper diet, enrichment toys
- Committing fully to pets before acquiring them
- Prioritizing pet welfare over personal gain
- Volunteering or donating to pet charities

Counteracting animal abuse, abandonment, neglect and commodification of pets should be urgent priorities. Pet influencers must awaken society's conscience, not just entertain it.

Final Thoughts: The Ethics of Pet Influencing

Pet influencing carries immense ethical obligations. At its core, upholding animal welfare, authenticity and honesty must remain central pillars for this community. Pet health can never be compromised for profit or fame.

But beyond just caring for their own pets, influencers now consider environmental impact and the broader promotion of animal rights. Their reach offers incredible potential to drive social change.

By embracing their roles as both entertainers *and* educators on pet ethics, these digital stars can help shape a more responsible culture of human-animal relationships. Pet influencers who inspire this shift will leave the most meaningful legacy.

FAQs on Pet Influencing Ethics

Should pet influencers refuse all opportunities for profit?

No, earning an income through pet social media is understandable for the time/effort involved. But profit goals should never supersede animal health or compromise integrity. Reasonable balance is key.

Don't pets enjoy being famous online?

Most pets do enjoy interacting with their owners during photoshoots and videos. But influencers must limit stressful scenarios, watch for signs of anxiety, and balance fame demands with pet well-being.

Aren't influencers raising awareness by showcasing exotic pets?

Promoting exotic pets like big cats, monkeys or wolves glosses over complex issues like wildlife conservation, public safety, humane captivity and perpetuating the exotic pet trade. Ethical implications should be carefully weighed.

Should influencers speak out on political issues like animal testing?

Influencers should feel comfortable advocating for issues aligned with ethical principles, like combatting cruel training/testing. But understanding impact on business relationships first is wise.

How can influencers spot sham pet products to avoid promoting?

Researching health claims, consulting vets, scrutinizing reviews and assessing a brand's overall transparency helps determine if products are legitimate or scams.

18

Advanced Photography and Videography Techniques

Capturing high-quality photos and videos of your pet influencer is essential for creating engaging social media content and building your personal brand. However, taking your visual content to the next level requires mastery of advanced techniques in photography, videography, lighting, editing, and storytelling. This chapter will provide an in-depth guide to elevating the quality of your influencer pet's visual content.

Elevating Visual Content Quality

Creating professional-level photography and videography of your pet takes practice and commitment to honing your skills. But with the right techniques, equipment, and a creative eye, you can produce visual content that wows your audience.

Professional Photography Tips

When it comes to professional pet photography, follow these tips:

- **Use a DSLR camera:** Invest in a digital SLR camera that allows for interchangeable lenses and manual exposure settings. This gives you the most control and highest image quality.
- **Master aperture, shutter speed, and ISO:** Learn how properly adjusting these core settings can dramatically affect your photos. A wider aperture creates blurred backgrounds, fast shutter speeds freeze action, and higher ISOs allow for low light shooting.
- **Employ the rule of thirds:** Position your pet subject according to the rule of thirds for balanced, engaging compositions. Imagine dividing your frame into thirds vertically and horizontally. Align elements along those lines or at intersection points.
- **Focus on the eyes:** Use a fast lens and shallow depth of field to make your pet's eyes razor sharp. As the windows to their soul, eyes draw viewers in emotionally.
- **Shoot during golden hours:** Photograph pets outdoors near sunrise or sunset when lighting is soft and warm for flawless illumination.
- **Utilize natural light:** Seek out and utilize flattering natural light indoors near windows and outside in shade or indirect sun. Avoid direct flash.
- **Try unique perspectives:** Photograph your pet from their level on the ground or slightly above to achieve more intimate, intriguing angles.

- **Use props and accessories:** Incorporate toys, costumes, backdrops, and other accessories to showcase your pet's personality and tell a story.
- **Practice patience:** Be ready for perfect moments and willing to take many shots to capture your pet at their best. Good pet photography requires time and persistence.

With practice implementing these tips, you can achieve professional quality pet influencer photography that engages your audience and builds your personal brand.

Advanced Videography Skills

Creating cinematic and professional-looking video content requires developing key videography skills:

- **Stabilize your shots:** Invest in camera stabilization tools like a gimbal or tripod for smooth, fluid camera movements. Shaky footage appears amateur.
- **Master composition:** Follow compositional guidelines like the rule of thirds and lead room to craft balanced, intentional shots.
- **Use multiple camera angles:** Vary wide, medium, and close-up angles to add visual interest and storytelling value to your video content.
- **Employ rack focusing:** Achieve a cinematic look by rack focusing between foreground and background elements during shots.
- **Incorporate slow motion:** Strategic use of slow motion to highlight cute mannerisms or action sequences can add production value.

- **Implement the 180-degree rule:** Maintain viewer orientation by keeping the camera on one side of the action to avoid disorientation.
- **Add b-roll:** Capture supplemental footage of environments, locations, props, and your pet in action for cutaway shots that enhance storytelling.
- **Control lighting:** Use natural light when possible or mount LED lights to evenly illuminate your pet and minimize shadows.
- **Ensure good audio:** Utilize directional microphones and reduce background noise for clear audio. Pay attention to sound quality.

With dedication to honing these advanced techniques, you can produce truly cinematic and professional-level videos that engage your pet influencer's audience.

Lighting and Composition Techniques

Proper lighting and photographic composition takes pet influencer visuals to the next level. Consider these tips:

- **Use soft, even lighting:** Soft, diffused lighting is most flattering for pets. Position them near large windows, outside under shade, or use a soft box light modifier indoors.
- **Craft intriguing compositions:** Utilize elements like leading lines, framing, geometric shapes, or the rule of thirds to make compelling images.
- **Shoot low angle:** Get on your pet's level and shoot upward for a sense of empowerment and personality.

- **Lens flare:** Backlight to intentionally create artistic lens flare and visually interesting highlights.
- **Reflections:** Compose shots with interesting mirrored reflections in water or glass to add depth.
- **Negative space:** Use empty space in the frame to draw attention to your focal point pet subject.
- **Patterns and textures:** Photograph your pet against backgrounds with appealing colors, patterns, or textures.
- **Symmetry:** Frame mirror-image compositions to showcase your symmetrical pet.
- **Leading lines:** Use diagonal lines like fences that point toward your pet subject to lead the viewer's eye.

Experimenting with these types of lighting techniques and compositional elements will elevate the visual interest of your pet photography and videography.

Editing and Post-Production Mastery

Meticulous editing and post-production can take your raw photos and footage to the next level. Implement these practices:

Editing Tools and Software

- **Use Lightroom:** Adobe Lightroom offers powerful editing tools for batch processing large quantities of photos quickly.
- **Try Luminar:** For AI-powered editing, Luminar can instantly improve photos with Enhance AI and unique filters.

- **Edit video in Premiere Pro:** For professional video projects, Adobe Premiere Pro provides robust tools, effects, and timeline editing features.
- **Utilize mobile apps:** For quick edits on the go, mobile apps like Adobe Lightroom or VSCO Cam offer handy editing capabilities.
- **Try desktop/mobile hybrids:** Software like Photoshop Express combines the power of desktop with the convenience of mobile for versatile editing.
- **Leverage presets:** Skip repetitive edits by creating and applying your own customized presets in Lightroom or VSCO.
- **Automate edits:** Use batch editing in Lightroom or editing actions in Photoshop to automate rote adjustments across multiple photos.

Choosing the right editing software that suits your needs and skill level is key to streamlining post-production.

Post-Production Best Practices

Follow these best practices when editing your pet influencer visual content:

- **Color grade for consistency:** Color grade photos and videos to create a consistent look and feel across your content.
- **Sharpen strategically:** Carefully sharpen areas only where needed to avoid an artificial look. Sharpen the eyes but avoid over-sharpening fur.
- **Selectively brighten:** Brighten underexposed areas and

subjects instead of indiscriminately overexposing every-thing.

- **Reduce noise:** Use noise reduction to minimize grain and unwanted texture while preserving detail.
- **Mask adjustments:** Make targeted adjustments by creating masks around specific portions of the image.
- **Match exposures:** Balance exposures across a series of photos by manually adjusting overly bright or dark images to match.
- **Review on multiple devices:** Preview your edits on both desktop displays and mobile devices to ensure they translate across screens.

Dedication to consistent, high-quality editing gives your content a refined, professional look that properly represents your brand.

Balancing Naturalism and Enhancement

When editing pet influencer visual content, aim for a nuanced balance between naturalism and enhancement. You want to highlight your pet's innate photogenic qualities while still creating beautiful, engaging imagery.

Some best practices include:

- **Preserve natural fur and eye color:** Avoid over-saturation and stay true to your pet's genuine colors.
- **Retain texture and detail:** Maintain fine details like whiskers and fur; don't eliminate "flaws" like scars or grey hairs that add character.
- **Edit lightly:** Use a delicate touch, especially with portrait

retouching. Don't overly smooth or liquify facial features.

- **Enhance expression:** Gently refine details around eyes and mouth to accentuate emoive expression.
- **Compliment naturally:** Play up existing positive qualities like vibrant eyes or a great smile. Don't radically alter appearance.
- **Focus on lighting:** Rely more heavily on great lighting setups vs. editing manipulations to create stunning photos.

With a nuanced approach that retains natural personality while still creating compelling imagery, you can produce content that feels authentic yet still visually engaging.

Storytelling Through Visuals

Beyond technical mastery, creating visual content that connects with audiences comes down to storytelling. Keep these narrative techniques in mind:

Crafting a Narrative With Images and Video

- **Establish a narrative arc:** Like a story, good visual content has a beginning, middle, and end with scenes sequentially building to a climax.
- **Show, don't only tell:** Rely on visuals to inform and emotions to persuade. Your audience should inherently understand the story you wished to convey through creative visual storytelling alone.
- **Include establishing shots:** Open with wide shots that introduce the location and situation to provide context.

- **Incorporate varied perspectives:** Switch between close-ups, medium shots, and wide angles to add layers and advance the story.
- **Use transitions carefully:** Cut between shots intentionally using transitions like fades, wipes or sound bridges to link scenes fluently.
- **End on a high note:** Close with a memorable final visual that leaves a lasting impact and encourages viewers to take action.

Emotional Engagement Through Visuals

- **Shoot candid moments:** Capture authentic interactions, spontaneous behavior, and unscripted emotions to elicit viewer empathy.
- **Leverage the eyes:** Channel personality and make an emotional connection through close-ups showcasing your pet's expressive eyes.
- **Use slow motion:** Highlight sweet or playful mannerisms in slow motion to create affection, sentimentality, or amusement.
- **Reveal the environment:** Let the location and surroundings visually reinforce the emotion or mood you wish to convey.
- **Include details:** Zoom in on small details like a gently wagging tail, twitching ear, or inquisitive expression that add personality.
- **Focus on interactions:** Show genuine bonds and rapport between pets and humans through engaging interaction shots.

Integrating Visuals with Overall Content Strategy

- **Align with your brand:** Ensure visuals authentically reflect your pet influencer's unique personality, life, and content style.
- **Support written content:** Use visuals that complement blogs and captions as visual evidence or to convey what words alone cannot.
- **Optimize for different platforms:** Tailor visual content to the unique formats of each social platform from square crops on Instagram to 9:16 vertical video on TikTok.
- **Promote engagement:** Ask questions or encourage viewers to participate in the story being told through your visual content to spark engagement.
- **Reinforce key messaging:** Align imagery with the broader narrative and messaging that you want to reinforce surrounding your personal brand as an influencer.
- **Monitor performance:** Pay attention to top-performing visual content themes and types. Then create more of what resonates most with your audience.

Strategically integrating visual storytelling with your broader content plan and brand identity ensures maximum engagement and impact.

Final Thoughts: Advanced Photography and Videography Techniques

Achieving photography and videography mastery involves continuous practice and learning. But dedicating yourself to honing your technical abilities, creative eye, editing skills, and visual storytelling techniques can help you produce truly stellar content.

Remember to always balance authenticity with enhancement when editing by emphasizing your pet's innate personality and charm. Stay true to who they genuinely are.

And keep experimenting with new styles, angles, props, lighting techniques, compositions, and perspectives. This will expand your creative horizons and keep your content feeling fresh.

Most importantly, ensure your visual content aligns strategically with your pet influencer brand identity and supports your broader content mission. Impactful storytelling requires coherence and purpose.

With advanced skills and a strategic approach, the visual content you create for your pet influencer will be eye-catching, compelling, and engaging on a professional level.

Frequently Asked Questions

Here are answers to some common questions about advanced pet influencer photography and videography techniques:

What camera is best for pet photography and videography?

For photography, a DSLR like a Canon or Nikon with interchangeable lenses provides the most control over image quality. For video, consider a mirrorless camera like the Sony A7S III with in-body stabilization.

How can I get better shots of fast-moving pets?

Increase your shutter speed to 1/500th second or faster, use continuous autofocus, choose a fast burst mode, and take many shots in a sequence to increase your chances of capturing crisp action.

What light works best for pet photography?

Soft, diffused natural light is most flattering. Indirect bright window light or outdoor shade are great sources. Avoid direct flash and harsh shadows.

How do I calm my pet for photos/videos?

Use positive reinforcement and treats to associate the camera with a reward. Work in short bursts and remain calm yourself. Stick to routines and schedules your pet is accustomed to.

What makes an engaging pet photo?

Great pet photos feature expressive eyes, intriguing perspectives, authentic moments, appealing lighting, engaging compositions, personality-revealing details, and a genuine emotional connection.

19

Leveraging Pet Influence for Social Causes

The age of social media has given rise to a new kind of celebrity - the pet influencer. Cute and cuddly cats, dogs, and even exotic animals have garnered millions of followers across platforms like Instagram, TikTok, and YouTube. But beyond just providing entertainment value, many prominent pet influencers are using their fame and reach for good. They actively leverage their brand and audience for social causes like animal welfare, wildlife conservation, and public education.

Advocacy and Awareness Campaigns

Pet influencers have a unique opportunity to utilize their platforms for advocacy and raising awareness on issues related to animal rights, pet ownership, and wildlife conservation. With an engaged audience passionate about animals, they can effectively promote these causes.

Supporting Animal Rights and Welfare

Many pet influencers collaborate with and promote non-profit organizations working towards animal rights and welfare. For example, the famous grumpy cat Lil Bub often shared adoption campaigns by shelters. Boo, the Pomeranian dog with over 16 million Facebook followers, frequently posts about supporting Guide Dogs for the Blind.

Other ways influencers support this cause is by speaking out against practices perceived as inhumane like dog meat farms, circus animal acts, and cosmetic animal testing. Activist campaigns aimed at ending the exploitation of exotic wild species as pets are also increasingly gaining celebrity endorsement. These endorsements lend credibility and signal boost vital conversations around animal ethics.

Raising Awareness on Pet-Related Issues

Influential pets have brought mainstream attention to several pet-centric issues that previously lacked awareness. For example, Lil Bub's unique physical attributes were due to genetic mutations causing dwarfism and polydactylism. This lent her a platform to raise awareness and funds for special needs rescue pets.

Education around reducing stray populations and promoting spaying/neutering has also gained more prominence. Pet obesity is another issue that influencers like Chloe the obese beagle have put the spotlight on. Their weight loss journeys educate people on providing optimal nutrition and exercise.

Overall, pets with large followings have successfully leveraged their unique circumstances to raise awareness on overlooked issues impacting animal health and welfare. Their relatable struggles make these causes more tangible and spur activism.

Collaborating with Non-Profits and Charities

Partnering with established non-profits gives influencer-led campaigns structure, resources and greater visibility. For instance, digital sensation Boo frequently collaborated with PETA for awareness drives on dog homelessness and pet adoption. The late keyboard cat worked with charities like RedRover for fundraising.

Celebrity pets have also been appointed as ambassadors for animal welfare organizations. For example, Lil Bub was named the first spokescat for the American Society for the Prevention of Cruelty to Animals (ASPCA). In this role, she headlined campaigns educating people on identifying and stopping pet abuse.

These partnerships allow non-profits to capitalize on the influencer's audience for fundraising and volunteer recruitment. On the other hand, it allows the pet to demonstrate social consciousness and further build brand image. Hence, it's a mutually beneficial way for charitable organizations and influencers to maximize their impact.

Educational Content Creation

Education is crucial for improving animal welfare. Pet influencers often utilize their platforms to create informational content that promotes responsible pet ownership.

Informing Audiences on Pet Care and Health

From nutrition to grooming, influencers regularly create educational content that provides value to pet owners. Health conditions like allergies, arthritis, dental hygiene, etc. are also addressed to expand awareness.

For instance, Maymo the lemon beagle's YouTube channel has tutorials on training tips and exercise routines for enrichment. Monty The Cat imparts care advice for feline health issues like urinary tract infections.

This content helps owners understand their pet's needs better and identify issues early for prompt veterinary care. It also informs prospective pet parents on duties required for responsible ownership beforehand.

Promoting Responsible Pet Ownership

Beyond just care instructions, influencers also utilize content to promote accountability in viewers. This includes emphasizing the need for following best practices like timely vet visits, spaying/neutering, microchipping, licensing, etc.

For example, george_the_giant on Instagram often reinforces through captions that giant breed dogs require extensive training and adequate living space. Chloe The Fat Beagle spreads awareness on ensuring pets maintain a healthy weight.

This content engages audiences by imparting practical wisdom from the pet's first-hand experiences. It helps potential adopters assess if they can realistically fulfill these lifelong responsibilities before getting a pet.

Collaborative Educational Initiatives

Some influencers have launched dedicated channels for instructional content beyond just social media posts. An example is Crusoe the Celebrity Dachshund's self-titled YouTube channel with 400K+ subscribers. It offers training tutorials, product reviews, advice videos and more catered to dachshund owners.

Collaborations are also common - Lil Bub hosted an educational video series with Animal Planet on pet wellness and animal ethics. Partnerships with veterinarians, trainers and brands allow influencers to create specialized content that engages and informs viewership.

Overall, education is a pivotal way for influencers to create social impact by empowering pet owners with actionable knowledge. The sheer diversity of platforms permits disseminating information through diverse formats like blogs, videos, live talks and podcasts.

Community Involvement and Volunteering

Beyond just digital activism and content, pet influencers actively contribute resources and time towards community animal welfare efforts. Their involvement inspires fans to also participate.

Participating in Community Events

Influencers often participate in local events to connect with followers. For example, pet expos, fundraisers, adoption fairs and shows provide opportunities to promote their brand while engaging in public outreach for causes.

Booths at such events allow fans to meet celebrity pets up close. The influencer presence also boosts overall event attendance and fundraising potential for organizers. For instance, Marnie The Dog regularly hosted acclaimed meet and greet booths at prominent ComicCons before passing away in 2020.

Ultimately, community participation generates goodwill, entertains animal lovers locally, and channels the influencer's appeal into social impact.

Organizing Fundraisers and Drives

Influential pets may headline and promote fundraising campaigns for animal welfare non-profits. Generally done through partnerships, these campaigns finance important initiatives like fostering rescue animals, sterilization drives and building shelters.

For example, Doug The Pug holds an annual holiday fundraiser selling limited edition merchandise. Proceeds support organizations like the Nashville Humane Society. Nala Cat organizes an annual 'Nala's Giving Tuesday' fundraiser for financial aid for owners facing hardship.

Such initiatives allow super-fans to directly aid causes dear to their favorite pet celebrities. Influencers amplifying these drives within their network maximizes reach and contributions.

Volunteer Work with Animal Shelters

Hands-on volunteer work at community animal shelters is another way pet influencers give back. Tasks can include walking and socializing animals, administrative work, assisting in veterinary clinics, outreach at adoption drives etc.

For instance, celebrities like TinyKittens and Voodoo The Samoyed volunteer extensively with local cat and dog shelters respectively. These efforts directly improve quality of life and adoption odds for rescues besides raising awareness generally.

Volunteering also allows influencers to lead by example and motivate fans to contribute their time and skills as well. Passionate viewers inspired by celebrity pets they admire can become powerful advocates themselves within their own communities.

Final Thoughts on Leveraging Pet Influence for Good

Famous pets with digital platforms have a special opportunity to drive real social impact. Their sheer reach and engaged viewers make them influential advocates for animal welfare and education. While these pets attain fame primarily through their cutesy content, it is uplifting to see many also leverage their privilege to enact substantive change.

Sure, these pets have agents, managers and entire PR teams orchestrating their fame. But that does not diminish the immense awareness they have brought to overlooked issues. These celebrity animals have empowered countless regular pet owners with better knowledge as well. Through fundraising drives and direct outreach, they have mobilized resources that have tangibly improved lives.

While critics may dismiss pet influencers as just fluffy vehicles for mindless entertainment, their earnest charity work reveals their true commitment as agents of social good. Their efforts inspire their millions of admirers to also participate in community animal welfare. Overall, pet influencers serve as excellent role models for what it takes to be a responsible, caring pet owner.

Frequently Asked Questions about Pet Influencers and Charity Work

How do pet influencers raise money for charity?

Common fundraising avenues include selling limited edition merchandise, organizing donation drives, and promoting non-profit campaigns through social media. Influencers may also headline or host events where ticket fees benefit charities. Their participation boosts attendance and contributions.

What charities do pet influencers support?

Popular charities include the ASPCA, PETA, Best Friends Animal Society, shelters, special needs pet rescues, and foundations funding medical treatment for pets in need. Local community shelters are commonly supported through volunteering and fundraising drives as well.

How can followers participate in a pet influencer's charity work?

Followers can participate by donating to fundraising drives, purchasing charity merchandise, attending events, volunteering at shelters after being inspired, and spreading awareness about campaigns through their own networks. Tagging the influencer when participating amplifies the message further.

Why should pet influencers do charity work?

Pet influencers have a large, engaged audience passionate about animals. Hence they have a unique opportunity to drive real impact on issues like homelessness, cruelty and neglect. Charity work also helps build a socially conscious brand image.

What are examples of famous pet influencers who do charity work?

Notable pet influencer activists include Lil Bub, Boo, Doug the Pug, Nala Cat, Chloe the Fat Beagle, Maymo the Lemon Beagle, and Crusoe the Celebrity Dachshund. Even exotic pets like monkeys and hedgehogs participate in advocacy today!

20

Innovative Monetization Strategies for Pet Influencers

Pets are big business. In the US alone, over $100 billion was spent on our furry friends in 2020. As a pet influencer, you have a massive opportunity to capitalize on this rapidly growing industry. But Gone are the days of relying solely on ad revenue and sponsorships. To build a sustainable business, you need to diversify your income streams.

This chapter will explore innovative ways pet influencers can monetize their brand beyond traditional methods. We'll cover creating digital products, subscription services, merchandise, affiliate marketing, long-term sponsorships, and more. With the right strategy, you can develop multiple pillars of revenue that empower you to do what you love, while still paying the bills.

Crafting Digital Products for Passionate Audiences

One of the most lucrative ways to monetize your influence is by creating digital products. These are non-physical items you sell to your audience, usually delivered digitally.

The great thing about digital products is that they can be created once, but sold indefinitely. The initial investment of your time pays off in the long run.

Here are some digital products worth considering:

Informational eBooks

Have in-depth knowledge on a pet-related topic? Package your expertise into an eBook and sell it on your website. For example, you could create:

- A training guide to teach puppies basic commands
- An eBook on homemade pet food recipes
- A pet first aid handbook

Use your influence to promote the eBook to your audience on social media and in videos.

Online Courses

Take your eBook idea further by turning it into a comprehensive online course. Use video lessons, worksheets, Q&As and other materials to create an immersive learning experience.

Online courses allow you to charge a higher price point, often $100+. The value comes from ongoing access and interactive elements.

Prestige Coaching and Mentorships

For pet influencers with extensive expertise, coaching and mentorships are ultra premium offerings. These provide 1-on-1 guidance and support from you.

Given the exclusivity, you can charge $500+ per month for this level of access. Limit spots to deliver a high-touch service.

Downloadable Pet Care Printables

Create value-packed printables like pet feeding schedules, training logs, health charts, and more. These appeal to pet parents seeking convenient tools.

Sell printable PDF bundles on Etsy or your website for $5 to $20. This provides buyers with instant digital downloads.

The key is choosing digital products that solve problems for your target audience. Get inside their heads and address frustrating pain points.

Building Recurring Revenue With Subscription Services

Subscription services provide reliable recurring revenue. Instead of one-off purchases, members pay ongoing access fees for your product or service.

This gives you predictable income you can depend on month after month. Here are subscription models that work well:

Membership Sites

Behind a monthly "velvet rope", give members access to things like:

- Exclusive videos and blog content
- Discounts on your products/services
- Entry into member contests
- Ability to message you directly

The more value you provide, the more you can charge. $10 to $50 per month is typical.

Pet Box Subscriptions

Curate monthly themed boxes with your audience in mind. For example:

- Treats, toys and accessories for heavy chewers
- Products to pamper senior pets
- Gear for hiking/adventuring with dogs

Convenience is a major selling point of subscription boxes. Charge $30 to $60 per month for specialized themes.

Virtual Pet Coaching

Offer personalized pet coaching over video chat. This could be focused on areas like:

- Obedience training

- Leash walking manners
- Reducing pet anxiety

Charge per 30-60 minute session, or offer monthly packages. This leverages your expertise for recurring revenue.

Think about niche problems your audience struggles with. Craft subscriptions that cater specifically to those needs.

Creating Merchandise Pet Lovers Crave

Pet lovers want to proudly display their passion. Merchandise lets them do that, while providing you an income stream.

Let's explore creative merchandise ideas beyond just T-shirts:

Pet Bandanas

Super cute bandana designs make highly giftable merchandise fans love. Offer scarf sizes for cats and dogs of all sizes.

Bandanas can be affordably priced between $12 to $20 for healthy profit margins. These tend to sell particularly well.

Pet Parent Mugs and Water Bottles

Mugs, water bottles and other drinkware make great merchandise. Print funny pet sayings, cute art, or even pet photos on them.

Sell drinkware from your online shop for $15 to $25. These are items fans use daily.

Paw Print Jewelry

Jewelry imprinted with your pet's actual paw print design is personal and heartwarming.

Offer custom paw print pieces like necklaces, bracelets, keychains, and rings. Price these keepsakes from $30 to $75.

Pet Lover Apparel

Don't just slap logos on shirts and call it a day. Get creative with apparel like:

- Sweatshirts with pet hair emblazoned across it
- Socks printed with your pet's face all over
- Tank tops with fun pet owner sayings

Quality printed apparel can retail for $25 to $40.

New merchandise ideas are worth constantly testing and exploring. Don't just do what's expected. Wow pet lovers with creativity.

Leveraging Affiliate Marketing to Diversify Revenue Streams

Affiliate marketing is a smart way for pet influencers to earn commissions promoting relevant products.

Here are some tips to maximize affiliate revenue:

Choose Niche-Specific Programs

Instead of giant affiliate networks, find niche programs focused on pet products. This allows you to target promotions better.

For example, Ruff Life Pro is a leading pet-focused affiliate program. Their niche focus makes them ideal to partner with.

Authentically Integrate Affiliate Links

Don't overwhelm your audience with promotions. Organically mention affiliate products in contextually relevant spots.

For example, when writing a "daily walks with my dog" post, mentioning your favorite dog harness fits seamlessly.

Track Performance and Iterative

Use affiliate links with trackable codes so you can monitor their performance. Cut underperforming links, double down on winners.

This allows you to continually optimize, testing new links constantly and phasing out those with low conversion rates.

Affiliate marketing is never a primary revenue stream, but can provide noticeable supplementary income each month.

Securing Winning Sponsorships with Brands

Sponsorships involve getting paid by brands to promote their products or services. This is nothing new for influencers.

But meaningful long-term sponsorships require a more strategic approach. Follow these steps:

Research the Brand Thoroughly

Get to know a brand before reaching out. Understand their mission, audience and past influencer campaigns.

This allows you to pitch sponsorships tailored specifically to them. Generic copy/pasted proposals go ignored.

Craft a Custom Partnership Proposal

After researching the brand thoroughly, create a proposal outlining:

- Why their brand fits your audience and content
- Example integration ideas matching their goals
- Your audience demographics and user stats
- Examples of past successful partnerships

The proposal should highlight the value you will provide them and get them excited to work together.

Manage the Partnership Actively

Don't ghost brands after securing the deal. Maintain frequent communication and share content drafts and performance data.

Offer additional ways to amplify their products if things are going well. Become a trusted partner, not hired one-off talent.

Don't Just Stick to the Status Quo

Suggest creative ideas that take the partnership beyond their standard playbook. Come to the table with win-win activations they've never considered.

For example, when partnering with a dog food brand:

- Instead of just coupon codes, co-create a customizeable pet food formula for your audience
- Film a tour of their manufacturing facilities showing how they make food
- Talk to their head nutritionist and feature an interview on your blog

This shows you're willing to go the extra mile, helping them achieve more than typical influencer promos.

The brands who sponsor you should be ones you're genuinely excited about. Seek out partners doing innovative things in the pet space.

Final Thoughts on Monetizing Your Pet Influence

Launching new income streams beyond ad revenue alone can feel intimidating initially. But diversification is the path to building a viewer-supported business you control.

Start by identifying the biggest monetization opportunities based on your unique audience and strengths. Release your first digital product, merchandise collection or subscription offer. Progress may seem slow at first, but compounded over time you'll reach an inflection point.

Keep innovating new offerings while refining your strategy

based on data. Suddenly, you'll have built a thriving business aligned with your passion. Financial success is attainable if you expand beyond the expected.

Now it's your turn. Which of these monetization models resonates most? Look at your current audience and brand. Visualize what's possible, not just what's comfortable.

You have an unprecedented chance to turn your pet skills, knowledge and influence into income streams as unique as you are. Seize the opportunity while this industry is still growing.

The internet rewards those bold enough to take the first step, even if the path is unknown. I can't wait to see what you create.

Frequently Asked Questions

What is the most lucrative monetization model?

There is no universally "best" model. The most lucrative income stream for you depends on your unique audience, skills and interests. Testing different options is the only way to find out what resonates most.

How much should I charge for virtual pet coaching?

For 30 minute virtual coaching sessions, $35 to $60 is a typical price range. For 60 minute sessions, $60 to $100 per session is common. Offer packages of 5 or 10 sessions at a discounted rate to increase sales.

Should my merchandise be dropshipped or shipped from my own location?

Dropshipping through Print-on-Demand platforms can be great when first starting out and testing new merchandise. But long term, keeping merchandise in your own inventory allows higher profit margins and control over branding.

What percentage commission do most affiliate programs pay?

Commissions vary greatly between affiliate programs, but 5-15% per sale is typical. Some popular programs pay even higher commissions upwards of 25-30% for big-ticket items.

How many sponsorships deals should I aim for per year?

There's no perfect number, but most influencers shoot for 6-12 sponsored campaigns per year. This allows you to balance sponsored and non-sponsored content.

21

The Future of Pet Influencing

The world of pet influencing has exploded in popularity over the last decade. As social media opens up new opportunities for pets and their owners to build audiences and partner with brands, the potential impact of these animal influencers continues to grow. But in an industry driven by rapidly evolving technology and changing audience tastes, the future remains uncertain. What trends and innovations will shape pet influencing in the years to come? How can today's pet influencers future-proof their presence and longevity in an unpredictable landscape? This chapter explores emerging directions and strategies to equip pet influencers for continued success.

Predicting Future Trends in Pet Influencing

The pet influencing game is changing fast. As creators fight for a limited pool of audience attention and sponsorship deals, they need to closely track shifts in viewer preferences and platform algorithms. Actively researching developments in the wider influencer space provides valuable insight into what's next for the world of animal social media stars.

Several overarching trends stand out as likely to shape pet influencing in the future:

The rise of short-form vertical video: With the explosive growth of TikTok and Instagram Reels, short-form vertical videos are now massively popular. Pet influencers who embrace this format and optimize content for mobile screens stand to benefit enormously. Expect to see more ads and sponsorships seamlessly integrated into this style of video.

Live, raw, and real: Audiences increasingly crave behind-the-scenes authenticity from the influencers they follow. Pet accounts that incorporate livestreams, spontaneous in-the-moment videos, and raw footage can build deeper parasocial relationships with viewers. Showing the spontaneous moments in a pet's daily life helps humanize animal influencers.

Education and pet care advice: How-to tutorials and pet care education represent a major opportunity area for pet influencers in the future. As viewers look to social media for information, influencers who position themselves as knowledgeable experts on animal health, training, nutrition and more can attract huge audiences.

Focus on pet personalities and narratives: At its core, the appeal of following pet influencers lies in connecting with fun animal personalities. Accounts that strategically craft entertaining narratives and character arcs around a pet stand out. The future lies in storytelling and building distinct pet personas.

Growth of pet influencer teams and agencies: Running a successful pet influencer account is demanding. As the industry matures, expect to see more collaboration and the rise of dedicated teams or agencies supporting individual pet influencers. This allows for more polished branding and content.

Rise of pet influencer collectives: Collaboration will also drive growth through pet influencer collectives, where multiple accounts leverage combined audiences. Joint initiatives like Welp or Yappy allow for crossover promotions and partnerships.

Humanization through language and marketing: Applying human traits, emotions and language to animal influencers makes them more relatable. The strategic anthropomorphizing of pets will increase, as will products and brands tailored to their new "lifestyles".

Expanded and niche audiences: While broad appeal remains important, niche pet influencing for focused audiences offers room for growth. Expect rising pet influencers targeting specific demographics like parents, geographic regions, or pet types.

Specialization in pet verticals: Similarly, pet influencers covering narrower verticals and interests will thrive. For example, outdoor adventure dog accounts, cat fashion experts, or exotic pet caregivers. Specialization allows for targeted sponsorships.

Rise of pet merchandising: As brands realize the marketing potential of pet influencers, developing merchandise and products related to popular animal accounts will increase. Pet clothing lines, toys, pet food brands and more can launch off influencer personas.

Focus on sustainability: Eco-conscious messages and planet-friendly practices will be increasingly central to pet influencers' brand identities. This ties into consumers' growing sustainability concerns. Prioritizing ethics and green initiatives is the future.

This is just a sample of the many evolving trends to expect. The keys will be flexibility, knowing core audiences, and smartly adapting content to emerging platforms and formats. With so many moving pieces, predicting the future is difficult - but actively working to shape it is the job of forward-thinking pet influencers.

Adapting to New Technologies and Platforms

Of course, nailing social media trends is only one piece of the puzzle. Pet influencers also need to rapidly embrace new technologies that open up creative opportunities for content and engagement. Innovative tech creates avenues to stand out while allowing influencers to flex their skills and build deeper audience connections.

Interactive mobile apps like TikTok and Instagram Reels won't be the last viral sensations. Pet influencers should consistently scout emergent platforms, understanding their features and possibilities early. Becoming a top creator on a new app in its infancy stages can provide massive growth.

AI video generation tools are also unlocking new potential. For example, tools like Synthesia allow creating realistic animal avatars that can be animated to lip sync and act out customized videos. As the technology improves, expect AI-generated animal content to start going viral.

AR filters and lenses present fun opportunities for engagement and spontaneity too. Whether basic Instagram filters or more advanced Snapchat and TikTok lenses that track body movements, these can allow new types of playful pet content.

Influencers able to master viral AR will pull huge viewership.

Livestreaming adoption will further increase as platforms make streams accessible and interactive. Pet influencers should capitalize both through real-time broadcasting of events and milestones as well as scheduled streams that let viewers actively chat and engage.

Emerging wearable tech, like cameras, microphones, sensors, and trackers for pets can also enable new types of content. First-person point of view footage from a pet's perspective offers an immersive experience for viewers. Data analytics unlock real insights too.

Drone and gimbal camera advancements translate into higher production quality content and cinematic shots. As the tech gets cheaper and easier to use, it can help pet influencers produce uniquely captivating videos.

5G and high-bandwidth networks will support richer content formats like 360-degree video, VR, and volumetric video in the future. Ultra high definition and seamless streaming open new creative possibilities.

Of course, pinpointing specific emerging technologies is nearly impossible given the rapid pace of innovation. The key is maintaining awareness of the wider landscape and being quick to understand how new tools can enhance a pet influencer's content and audience engagement.

Experimentation with each tech trend is important - even if an innovation ends up as a short-lived fad, mastering it early often leads to valuable skills, sponsorships and authority. Adapting to both new platforms and cutting-edge tools is mandatory for continued relevance and growth as a pet influencer.

Innovating with AR, VR and AI

Two emerging technologies warrant particular focus given their potential to transform digital content: augmented reality (AR), virtual reality (VR), and artificial intelligence (AI). Their applications for pet influencing are vast - both now and even more so in the future.

Captivating Viewers with Augmented Reality

AR overlays digital elements onto the real world, creating dynamic and interactive content. Some examples of current AR uses for pet influencers:

- Fun AR lenses/filters/effects featuring or interacting with a pet
- AR stickers and objects added to photos or videos
- Immersive AR stories and games featuring a digital pet avatar
- AR apps to virtually try on pet accessories and products
- Educational AR content teaching pet care techniques in 3D

The technology is already widely popular on mobile platforms like Instagram, Snapchat and TikTok. But as AR hardware improves, we'll see adoption expand massively. AR glasses will eventually allow persistent overlays onto real world views. Spatial AR anchored in physical spaces will bring digital animal avatars and objects into any environment.

Early-adopting pet influencers who build skills with existing AR tools will be best positioned to capitalize on new applications in engaging and viral content. The opportunities to connect with audiences through innovative AR are endless.

Transporting Viewers with Virtual Reality

VR creates completely digital immersive worlds users can interact with and explore. Current options for pet influencers are limited - but the tech's trajectory points to huge future potential. Imagine:

- Lifelike VR videos allowing viewers to play with or care for a pet influencer in virtual reality
- VR stories from a pet's perspective, experienced firsthand from their point of view
- VR worlds featuring a digital pet avatar viewers can directly engage with
- Social metaverse hangouts in VR where fans can virtually hang out with a pet in real-time
- VR pet care simulations for training and education

As VR platforms and tools become more accessible and VR headsets decline in price, expect immersive virtual reality content to take off. Pet influencers who become early creators in VR will ride this wave. The level of engagement and connection from VR storytelling and environments outpaces any other medium.

Enhancing Content with Artificial Intelligence

AI is revolutionizing what's possible in content creation and audience engagement. Pet influencers who embrace AI tools gain an advantage. Areas to watch include:

AI-generated text & audio: Advanced natural language algorithms can craft written captions, scripts, and blog posts as well as generate realistic voiceovers in a pet's verbal style. This automates and scales up content production.

AI-powered video editing & effects: Editing tools utilizing AI will speed up stitching footage, color correcting, adding graphics and text, and more. Specialized AI effects will be customizable for animals.

AI avatars: As mentioned, artificial intelligence can create animated 3D avatars of pets that viewers deeply connect with. These can be used for all video and metaverse content.

AI recommendations: Algorithmic recommendations already drive a massive amount of viewer discovery and retention. Optimizing content strategies for evolved AI matching systems will be mandatory.

AI profile and sentiment analysis: AI can help analyze audience data, comments, and responses to give pet influencers valuable insights into their followers. This allows better understanding their needs.

Predictive audience targeting: Advanced analytics AI can support predicting which viewers are most likely to take key actions like sharing content, buying merchandise or engaging with sponsors. Influencers can then target content appropriately.

The possibilities are endless. Integrating artificial intelligence thoughtfully at every stage from content creation to audience analysis can transform engagement. Pet influencers who strategically tap into emerging AI have an advantage in reaching and resonating with viewers.

Reaching International Audiences

A huge opportunity lies in expanding beyond domestic audiences to tap into the global pet-loving community. While crossover social media hits can always go viral internationally, deliberately localizing efforts is key for lasting worldwide growth.

Pet owners' fundamental love for their animals crosses cultures. However, influencers need to consider a few factors to adapt their content and branding appropriately for different regions.

Adapting Content for Global Appeal

The visual content itself often requires little adaptation. Funny or cute animal moments appeal universally!

However, pet influencers should consider:

- **Translating captions and text** into diverse languages. Auto-translate makes this quick but having native speakers proofread is ideal.
- **Avoiding pop culture references** or slang that may not translate. Stick to universal themes and emotions.
- **Showcasing local languages.** Incorporate visual snippets featuring the pet interacting with common regional phrases and imagery.
- **Researching regional pet care norms** and trends to

tap into. What humanization, accessories, practices or terminology resonate in different cultures?

- **Adding culturally relevant details** like backgrounds, music, food or traditions. These nuances make content feel locally authentic.
- **Captioning videos** for accessibility, which varies across regions.
- **Adhering to regional content rules and restrictions.** Be aware of what's permitted on each platform in a given country.

The goal is maintaining the core pet personality and brand while adapting the framing, details and text for relevance in each market. Localizing content opens the pet influencer up to massive new audiences.

Collaborating with International Brands

Just as important as adapting content is partnering with brands relevant in local markets. This often involves identifying and pitching:

- **Pet brands popular only in specific regions.** Local pet food, toy or accessory brands have built-in audiences.
- **Larger international brands' regional divisions or campaigns.** A global brand's India branch likely wants India-specific content.
- **Country-specific platforms** like WeChat in China or VKontakte in Russia. Partnering with dominant local networks is valuable.
- **Language-targeted campaigns** from global brands. For

example, a Spanish shampoo ad for Hispanic markets.

- **Culture-specific occasions and events.** Chinese New Year sponsorships resonate in Asian markets, for instance.
- **International pet holidays.** Like National Dog Day in the US or International Cat Day for global campaigns.
- **Travel and tourism partnerships** in each region. Pitching travel brands hasbuiltin appeal.

The goal is collaborating with brands authentically rooted in each local market. This allows sponsored content that engages new international audiences while being revenue-generating. Think globally, act locally.

Adapting to Changing Social Media Landscapes

One certainty about social platforms is that they will change. What's hot one year becomes outdated the next. Early MySpace pioneers can tell you all about lost followers.

Succeeding as a pet influencer over the long-term means riding the waves of trends and platform evolution. Some strategies include:

Maintaining diverse social presences across multiple platforms so your engaged audience is not tied to any one. Losing followers on Instagram isn't devastating if you have thriving accounts on YouTube, TikTok, Twitter and more.

Closely monitoring metrics and audience engagement signals on each platform. Identify changes early and adapt strategies accordingly. Jump ship from declining platforms in time.

Experimenting with emergent niche apps before they go

mainstream. Build authority and followers from the ground up if they take off.

Not over-relying on ephemeral viral hits alone. Those bring short-term gains but developing recurring audience relationships leads to longevity.

Balancing established and innovative content formats based on each platform's algorithm shifts and popularity. Give audiences what they want but also what they didn't know they wanted.

Researching updates and best practices for each platform algorithm regularly. Update strategies accordingly, while still maintaining an authentic brand identity.

Collaborating with influencer collectives to diversify reach across multiple engaged audiences and accounts. Share knowledge and strategies for navigation.

Emphasizing audience relationships and community building above simple follower counts. Loyal brand fans will stick around regardless of platform changes. Engagement is the real metric for success.

With social media's fast-changing nature, influencers can't afford to stand still. The pets with staying power will be those proactively making moves to capitalize on platform trends both old and new.

Evolving Your Pet's Brand Over Time

A common pitfall for any influencer who achieves some success is getting stuck simply repeating what worked before. Complacency breeds creative staleness and audience drop-off.

Top pet influencers stay fresh by intentionally evolving

their brand, image and content over time. Think of the pet's brand journey like a story arc.

Some tips:

Map out distinct life/story stages for the pet aligned to their aging and changing lifestyle. Playful puppy hijinks can transition to travel photoshoots with an adventurous adult dog.

Level up production value and creativity each year. Growth of skills and budget should translate into tangible improvements in content.

Expand into new platforms and content formats as they emerge, while closing deprecated accounts. Meet audiences where they are.

Introduce new pet characters like siblings, friends or babies to keep the narrative interesting. Spin-off accounts can help too.

Spot trends and realign content to capitalize on what's hot while retaining the core brand.

Find creative new angles on recurring content types like reaction videos or pet holiday photos. Even established formats can stay fresh.

Develop new personality facets, catchphrases, or backstories that add dimensionality over time. Acquire an interest in art. Share witty musings.

Collaborate with diverse co-stars like family members, famous pets, or niche celebrities to spark interest.

Refresh visual brand elements like logos, color schemes, graphics, and editing styles for a new era. Change welcomes new audience interest.

Pet influencers who simply recycle the same old tricks start feeling one-note. Intentionally evolving the pet's narrative and image keeps fans engaged over the long haul. Think long-term story arcs.

Preparing for the Future of Pet Influencing

Given the influencer industry's unpredictability, nobody can say exactly what pet influencing will look like 5 or 10 years down the line. But the pets best positioned to succeed will be those who:

Remain nimble and open-minded to embrace emergent trends, platforms, tech and partnerships

Commit to steady learning and upskilling in creative content production and marketing

Build authentic emotional connections with fans that transcend superficial vanity metrics

Focus on personality and storytelling above all else to drive meaningful engagement

Monitor audience data and feedback to continually fine-tune content strategies

Cultivate a bold creative vision unafraid to experiment with innovative content formats and styles

Collaborate extensively with fellow pet influencers to benefit from shared knowledge

Structure smart monetization models with diversified income streams and sponsorships

Never lose sight of their pet's wellbeing, ensuring social media work stays positive and ethical

This foundation sets up pet influencers to roll with whatever the future holds - and even help shape it.

The world of animal social media stars holds infinite potential still to be unlocked. As emerging technologies empower new possibilities and creative formats to reach audiences, pet influencers must embrace the unknown. With smart evolution, authenticity and courage to take risks, their bonds with dedicated fans can only grow in strength. The future remains unwritten - and that's thrilling.

Final Thoughts: The Future of Pet Influencing

The path ahead promises massive opportunities for pet influencers willing to evolve and innovate. By predicting trends, mastering fresh technologies, expanding reach, collaborating, and crafting compelling stories, animal social media stars can future-proof their presence. Maintaining authenticity and adaptability will allow today's pet influencers to ride whatever waves come their way next. The influences of tomorrow will be those that

22

Pet Influencer Networking and Collaboration

Gone are the days when influencers worked in isolation. In today's connected world, building strategic partnerships and networking with other creators is essential for taking your pet influencer career to the next level. Collaborating with fellow influencers allows you to expand your reach, participate in larger campaigns, gain exposure, and share valuable resources. However, networking successfully requires strategy and finesse. This chapter provides actionable tips for pet influencers looking to develop impactful professional relationships and working synergies. Let's dive in!

Building Strategic Partnerships

Forging partnerships with compatible influencers is one of the most effective ways to boost your growth and credibility. But how do you identify the right collaborators? And what makes for a mutually beneficial alliance? Here are some tips:

Identifying Potential Collaborators

When seeking potential partners, look for influencers who are in a similar niche but have differentiated content and follower demographics. This way you can expand each other's reach instead of just preaching to the same choir.

Some important factors to consider:

- **Niche compatibility:** Partner with influencers in adjacent pet niches like cat influencers as a dog influencer. This allows you to tap into each other's highly engaged audiences.
- **Non-overlapping followers:** Analyze follower overlap using social media analytics tools. Look for under 25% overlap for maximum incremental reach.
- **Complementary content styles:** Partnering with an influencer with a different aesthetic and content approach brings diversity and novelty for both audiences.
- **Differing geographic followers:** Influencers with audiences concentrated in different countries or regions unlock new markets.
- **Distinct social media footprint:** Cross-promoting an influencer dominant on a different platform like YouTube broadens distribution.
- **Reputation and work ethic:** Vet potential partners thoroughly and ensure you align on professionalism. Arising tide lifts all ships.

Cast a wide net during your search process before narrowing down on a shortlist of ideal collaborators. Thoroughly explore their content and brand before reaching out.

Forming Mutually Beneficial Partnerships

The key to a successful collaboration is structuring the partnership so that both parties stand to gain clear benefits. Be explicit about objectives and incentives from the outset.

Some potential win-wins to consider:

- **Audience expansion:** Cross-promote each other's content and accounts to tap into new follower bases.
- **Campaign participation:** Join forces as co-creators on branded influencer campaigns to qualify for larger and more exclusive opportunities.
- **Resource and knowledge sharing:** Exchange industry insights, tools, or access to various professional services.
- **Skills development:** If one excels on TikTok and the other on Instagram Reels, collaborate to gain cross-platform skills.
- **Geographic expansion:** Help each other create localized content tailored for new target countries or regions.
- **Creative inspiration:** Brainstorming sessions can catalyze fresh content ideas for both parties.
- **Cost savings:** Split costs for accessories, tools, professional services, travel etc. to benefit from bulk pricing.

Discuss objectives, incentives, and performance metrics openly when structuring the partnership framework. Outline promotional activities, campaign collaboration details, and resource sharing specifics early on.

Collaborative Content Creation

One of the most exciting aspects of influencer partnerships is co-creating content together. This allows each creator to put their unique spin on a collaboration while exposing their audience to new, dynamic material.

When co-producing content:

- **Ideate complimentary concepts:** Develop content themes and storylines that play to both creators' strengths and niches.
- **Align on formats:** Determine the best formats for collaboration content - vlogs, reels, TikToks etc based on audience preferences.
- **Co-develop production plans:** Map out roles, responsibilities, timelines, and logistics. Who will conceptualize? Who will edit? Who takes the lead at each stage?
- **Match aesthetics:** While styles may differ, ensure visual components like filters, music etc. flow together.
- **Bridge content:** Create transitory clips announcing the collaboration and teasing exciting future videos.
- **Cross-promote extensively:** Preview, release and amplify the content across both accounts.
- **Track performance:** Monitor view counts, engagement, follower growth and other metrics to optimize future collaborations.

With aligned objectives, incentives, and content strategies - influencer collaborations can be incredibly rewarding for all involved.

Networking at Industry Events

Industry conferences and events provide unparalleled networking and partnership opportunities. Pet influencer gatherings like VidCon, Playlist Live and Petcon give creators access to fellow influencers, brands, press and platform reps. Here's how to maximize the experience:

Maximizing Opportunities at Conferences

Success at events is about meticulous preparation, proactive outreach, and maximizing your time onsite. Some tips:

- **Research attendees:** Identify ideal collaborators and connection targets who will be present.
- **Schedule meetings:** Email high-priority contacts to set up meetings in advance. Don't rely solely on spontaneous networking.
- **Prepare pitches:** Craft personalized elevator pitches highlighting your value proposition for each key contact.
- **Develop content concepts:** Brainstorm co-creation ideas tailored to potential partner's niche and audience. Come prepared with win-win proposals.
- **Bring giveaways:** Having small branded items on hand helps make memorable impressions and incentivizes follow-ups.
- **Charge devices:** Carry portable chargers and cables so you never miss connectivity opportunities due to low phone battery.
- **Dress for confidence:** Make sure your outfit aligns with your personal brand and exudes professionalism.

With preparation and initiative, conferences provide the perfect atmosphere for planting the seeds of fruitful future partnerships.

Effective Networking Strategies

To maximize your impact at influencer events, mindfulness and strategy separates the veterans from the newcomers. Consider these tips:

- **Circulate with purpose:** Don't cling to acquaintances. Politely exit conversations to explore event and meet new people.
- **Warm introductions:** Connectors who can facilitate valuable introductions are golden. Seek them out. Offer to return the favor.
- **Listen intently:** Hear influencers' pain points and challenges. Offer relevant advice and solutions.
- **Follow-up relentlessly:** Collect contact info and connect on social media. Follow-up within 48 hours post-event.
- **Provide value:** Share insights, advice and ideas freely. Don't approach conversations self-servingly.
- **Stand out memorably:** Have a signature giveaway item, QR code, or conversation talking point.
- **Avoid desperation:** Convey passion and interest, but avoid conveying neediness at all costs. Exude abundance.
- **Highlight compatibility:** Emphasize niche and audience synergies when proposing partnerships. Visualize success.

With an intentional, value-driven approach - industry events offer unmatched relationship-building potential.

Building a Professional Network

Major events represent great opportunities to expand your professional network. But continued nurturing and engagement is crucial post-conference.

Some tips for network development:

- **Organize contacts:** Track all new connections in a CRM system like HubSpot for organized follow-up.
- **Schedule check-ins:** Set calendar reminders to check-in with key contacts to sustain momentum post-event.
- **Cross-promote content:** Share relevant content from new connections and ask them to reciprocate to keep building audience overlap.
- **Propose content collaborations:** Pitch one or two co-creation ideas tailored to each potential partner's niche.
- **Provide value freely:** Send newly connected influencers and brands relevant tips, articles or other helpful resources proactively.
- **Leverage connectors:** Ask event acquaintances who know key targets for warm introductions to short-circuit relationship building.
- **Give before you get:** Build authentic relationships vs transactional ones. The payback will come indirectly down the road.

With consistent nurturing and value-driven engagement, conference contacts can morph into key professional alliances over time. Put in the work.

Leveraging Influencer Networks

In addition to one-on-one partnerships, tapping into established influencer networks and communities represents a powerful networking strategy. These groups and forums allow for broader collaborations.

Joining Influencer Groups and Forums

Many organizer groups cater specifically to influencers by niche like pet, travel or food. Here are some benefits of joining influencer networks:

- **Group campaign collaborations:** Multiple influencers work together on branded campaigns as a collective.
- **Community support system:** Discuss challenges and receive advice from those who've been there.
- **Platform connections:** Organizer reps provide training, tools, beta access and support.
- **Leverage founder expertise:** Group founders are often industry vets who mentor emerging influencers.
- **Broaden reach:** Participate in member takeovers and co-promotion activities.

While some groups are free, those with greater benefits often charge monthly membership fees. Thoroughly vet any group before joining to ensure legitimate value.

Collaborating on Larger Campaigns

Influencer networks provide access to larger scale brand partnership activations involving groups of creators. This allows you to:

- **Access bigger opportunities:** Collaborative campaigns often have higher compensation and scope.
- **Gain exposure to major brands:** Household name brands seek group activations to maximize reach.
- **Increase discoverability:** New followers exposed to the campaign may engage with your personal brand.
- **Acquire key skills:** Develop competencies around pitching, contracting, collaborating and delivering on larger campaigns.
- **Build credibility:** Being hand-selected elevates your brand authority and trust.

When participating in group work, maintain alignment with fellow influencers while putting your distinctive spin on deliverables. It's still about showcasing your unique value.

Sharing Resources and Insights

In addition to collaborations, influencer networks allow creators to exchange valuable resources, knowledge and data. Some ways to contribute value within groups:

- **Share trending topics:** Keep other members updated on rising themes and platforms in your niche.
- **Highlight effective campaigns:** Provide behind-the-

scenes insights into your most successful activations.

- **Review services and tools:** Provide honest reviews of various apps, software, or services relevant to influencers.
- **Analyze performance data:**Participate in group data analysis by sharing anonymized traffic and engagement metrics.
- **Showcase processes:** Walk through your workflows for content creation, editing etc and invite discussion.
- **Give back:** Mentor less experienced influencers in the group through providing feedback and guidance.

The sense of community and willingness to share makes groups rewarding both professionally and personally for pet influencers.

Final Thoughts: Pet Influencer Networking

Developing partnerships and professional connections with fellow pet influencers provides immense opportunities for growth. But collaborations must be strategic. Identify partners whose offerings complement yours for maximum synergy. Structure relationships around mutual benefit, always bringing value to the table. Conferences and influencer networks offer additional avenues for high-value relationship building within a larger community. Prioritize networking consistently, authentically, and proactively. Our pack is stronger together.

FAQs About Pet Influencer Networking

What are the benefits of networking for pet influencers?

Key benefits include expanding reach through cross-promotion, participating in collaborative campaigns, gaining knowledge, building credibility, and accessing opportunities.

What events are best for pet influencer networking?

Top events include VidCon, Playlist Live, Petfluencer Networking Bash, and niche-specific conferences like CatCon and SuperZoo.

How do I make networking conversations meaningful and memorable?

Focus on listening, providing value, and conveying genuine interest in collaborating. Have a signature icebreaker and follow-up within 24 hours.

How do I identify the right influencer partners for collaborations?

Look for compatible niches but differentiated content styles and non-overlapping audiences. Thoroughly vet potential partners on professionalism and work ethic.

What are some mutually beneficial incentives for influencer partnerships?

Cross-promotion to expand reach, co-created content, campaign collaborations, geographic expansion, resource sharing, and cost savings.

23

Personal Branding and PR for Pet Influencers

Developing a Strong Personal Brand

As a pet influencer, your personal brand is everything. In many ways, *you* are the product - your personality, your lifestyle, your unique content. Without a compelling personal brand, it's impossible to stand out amongst the crowded space of pet influencers fighting for followers and sponsorships. A strategic, thoughtful approach to crafting your brand identity and consistently reinforcing it across channels is essential to success.

Crafting a Unique Personal Brand Identity

Start by getting crystal clear on who you are and what makes you different. As a pet parent influencer, what is your unique perspective and passion? Do you have an inspiring adoption story? A knack for DIY dog toys? A talent for capturing your bunny's silly antics? Define your niche by reflecting on what you love about your pet and the type of content you enjoy creating.

Next, get to know your target audience. Who are you trying to reach? What are their interests and pain points? By understanding your ideal followers, you can shape content that provides value. Think about your brand's visual identity too. What image do you want to project? Choose design elements for your website and social media that express your personality and appeal to your audience.

Craft a brand mission statement and positioning to guide your efforts. For example, "Empowering new pet parents with positivity and playful tips" defines an uplifting brand purpose. Stay focused on your niche; generic content won't captivate anyone. Let your unique passion and perspective shine through.

Consistency in Brand Messaging

With a clear brand identity, remain utterly consistent in reinforcing it. Keep your website, captions, hashtags, and communication on-brand across platforms. Rethink content or partnerships that don't align. Say no to sponsorships that would compromise your mission. Nothing confuses followers more than a contradictory message.

Strike a balance between consistency and stagnation. As you evolve, refine your branding to reflect growth while retaining your core identity. Schedule regular check-ins to audit your messaging - is it still on target? Keep innovating within your niche to combat a stale personal brand.

Track your metrics to identify your best-performing content. Look for themes and trends to guide future posts. Lean into what resonates while pruning what doesn't. Consistency, not conformity, will amplify your impact.

Personal Branding Across Channels

With so many platforms available, using each intentionally is key. Start with your website, the hub for all personal branding efforts. Optimize your site for keywords to improve SEO and drive traffic. Showcase your best content, mission statement, press features, and contact info prominently.

Dedicate social channels to different facets of your brand. For pet parent tips and product reviews, longer-form blog posts or YouTube videos work well. Use Instagram and TikTok for funny behind-the-scenes moments. Riff on viral trends to increase shareability. Cross-promote new content across your other profiles.

In your email list and direct outreach, cultivate an intimate sense of community. Share personal updates and give exclusive sneak peeks. Collaborate with niche micro-influencers to expand your reach. Seek sponsorships that further your brand positioning. With a thoughtful cross-channel approach, elevating your personal brand has no limits.

Effective PR Strategies

Beyond creating great content, pet influencers need to master PR to turbocharge their brand. By strategically managing media relationships, publicity opportunities, and reputation, influencers gain an edge. Let's dig into tactics for PR success.

Managing Media Relationships

Start by researching targeted media outlets and journalists relevant to your niche. Pet magazines, local news sites, mommy blogs - get a list going. Follow these on social media to get familiar with their content style and tone.

Prepare customized pitches explaining why your brand is newsworthy to each publication. Offer them value by suggesting specific articles featuring you and your pet. Provide sample imagery and content to showcase your expertise. Follow up on pitches with emails combining persistence and patience.

Once you secure features, promote them heavily on your own channels! Landing press validates your influencer status so celebrate wins when they come. Maintain these media relationships by occasionally suggesting new stories or tips. Become a trusted industry resource that outlets turn to again and again.

Crafting Press Releases and Media Kits

Press releases are another way to share major announcements like launching a product line or charity partnership. Distribute through PR wire services for widespread reach.

Include punchy headlines, compelling quotes, and powerful imagery. Follow established press release templates while customizing details for your unique story. Incorporate relevant keywords to help press releases get found online.

Prepare a media kit to send with pitches or upon request. Include an about section, FAQ, press releases, high-res photos and videos, and testimonials. Make downloading your kit from your website seamless for easy access.

Handling Publicity and Media Opportunities

As your brand grows, exciting publicity opportunities will arise. If approached for a TV or podcast interview, prepare talking points ahead of time. Highlight your expertise but don't be afraid to show personality too. Share fun behind-the-scenes stories that make you relatable.

When hosting influencer events, use the opportunity to create shareable content. Snap photos for Instagram, capture crowd reactions on TikTok, and go live on YouTube to generate buzz.

Finally, don't be afraid to reach out and create your own media opportunities! Look for local pet expos or contests to enter. Pitch your own web series or community initiatives. Own your story instead of waiting for someone else to give you a platform.

Reputation Management and Crisis Handling

For pet influencers under the public microscope, mindfully managing your reputation is non-negotiable. Be proactive with these reputation management tactics.

Monitoring Brand Reputation

Keep a close eye on what people are saying about your brand through keyword searches and social media listening. Set up Google Alerts to receive notifications on relevant mentions. Respond quickly to negative reviews to resolve issues. Report imposter accounts piggybacking off your brand's name.

Perform regular self-audits reviewing your online presence. Delete old posts that no longer fit your brand or could be misinterpreted. Take down any stolen or copyrighted content. Scrutinize affiliate partnerships and sponsors to avoid guilt by association. A little reputation maintenance goes a long way.

Responding to Crises and Controversies

Despite best efforts, influencers inevitably face criticism or controversy. When a crisis strikes, resist the urge to react defensively. Take a beat to assess the situation objectively. Consider valid critiques that can help you improve.

Draft a response owning up to any mistakes, showing accountability. Apologize sincerely, without caveats. If the issue reflects a broader problem, outline specific steps you will take to avoid repeat issues. Respond promptly across the platforms the issue arose. Transparency and vulnerability can diffuse backlash.

Avoid getting sucked into heated arguments online. Stick to the facts only. If tensions escalate, disabling comments temporarily helps calm things down.

Maintaining a Positive Public Image

Combat negativity with an abundance of positivity. Share your passion for pets through charitable initiatives. Collaborate with respected brands doing good work. Keep engaging thoughtfully with your community.

Post consistently to keep feeding the social media algorithm. Stay visible by pitching articles and appearing at relevant events. Seek credible media opportunities over controversial clickbait.

Owning your narrative proactively is better than reactively defending it. By diligently managing your reputation, controversy becomes the exception not the norm. Beginning each day from a place of integrity leaves the critics without a foothold. Kill them with kindness and creativity.

Final Thoughts: Personal Branding and PR Are Ongoing Journeys

Distilling your multi-faceted life into a polished personal brand is an evolving process. Finding confidence in your voice while compromising quality takes practice. But pet influencers willing to do the work reap the rewards, enjoying lucrative sponsorships, a loyal following, and fulfilling work.

With an insider's view of the pet influencer world, I hope this content provided tactical tips for establishing and elevating your personal brand. By crafting a unique identity, maintaining consistency, seizing publicity opportunities, and monitoring your reputation, your influence will flourish.

While daunting at times, building a personal brand also holds the promise of authentic human connection. By boldly sharing your passion with the world, people and pets draw comfort from your vulnerability. Now is the time to dig deep and define the story only you can tell.

Frequently Asked Questions

How can I stand out in a crowded niche?

Experiment until you find your distinctive voice - whether comedy, advocacy, education, or inspiration. Infuse your content with your unique origin story, perspective and talents. Consistently reinforce what differentiates your brand.

How much time does PR and branding take?

Expect to invest at least an hour a day developing content and outreach. Set up systems to streamline and automate where possible. View consistency as success, not size. With time, your brand grows organically.

How do I secure brand sponsorships?

Research brands that align with your niche and pitch creative, customized collaborations. Start small with micro-influencers to build credibility. Respond promptly and professionally to potential partners. Deliver measurable results to build trust over time.

Should I hire an agency?

If you can afford it, partnering with PR and brand strategists provides helpful expertise. Though cost-prohibitive for some, agencies offer connections and efficiencies worth the spend.

How vulnerable should I get online?

Share struggles and tough times thoughtfully, not over-exposing in ways you may later regret. Be authentic while protecting your mental health and privacy too. Draw boundaries around what you feel comfortable publicly sharing.

24

Advanced Social Media Marketing Techniques

Mastering Paid Advertising

Paid advertising on social media platforms like Facebook, Instagram, and Twitter can be an extremely effective way to reach new audiences and promote your pet influencer brand. However, executing successful paid campaigns requires in-depth knowledge of each platform's advertising tools and capabilities.

Utilizing Paid Social Media Campaigns

The first step in running effective paid social campaigns is determining your goals and key performance indicators (KPIs). Typical goals for pet influencer campaigns may include:

· Increasing brand awareness and reach

- Generating leads and conversions
- Driving traffic to your website or online store
- Promoting upcoming content or events

Once you've defined your campaign goals, you can use the various advertising options on each platform to target your ideal audiences:

- **Facebook Ads:** Allows targeting users by demographics, interests, behaviors, and detailed audience segments. Placement options include the News Feed, Instagram, Messenger, and Audience Network.
- **Instagram Ads:** Target users by age, gender, location, interests, behaviors, and past activity on Instagram. Ad formats include photo, video, carousel, Stories, and Explore placements.
- **Twitter Ads:** Target Twitter users by keywords, interests, behaviors, device usage, and more. Promoted Tweet and Promoted Trends placements available.

When setting up campaigns, be sure to utilize all available targeting and placement options to reach your desired audiences in the most relevant contexts.

Targeting and Retargeting Strategies

Strategic audience targeting is key to maximizing your ad spend on social platforms. Here are some proven targeting and retargeting strategies for pet influencer campaigns:

- **Interest-based Targeting:** Target users specifically interested in pets, animal rescue, cute animals, and specific pet breeds.

- **Geographic Targeting:** Target users located near you to promote local events or meetups.
- **Lookalike Audiences:** Use your custom audiences or existing followers to find new users with similar traits.
- **Behavioral Targeting:** Target users who have engaged with pet-related content online or visited pet websites.
- **Retargeting:** Re-engage users who have previously visited your website, social pages or interacted with your ads.

Layering multiple types of targeting and tailoring messaging for each audience will improve ad relevance and performance. Retargeting past visitors or engagers helps keep your brand top of mind.

Measuring Ad Campaign Effectiveness

To determine the success of your paid social efforts and optimize future campaigns, it's essential to actively measure and track performance. Important metrics to monitor include:

- **Impressions:** Number of times your ads are displayed. Assesses reach.
- **Clicks:** Clicks on your ads. Measures engagement.
- **CTR:** Click-through-rate (clicks/impressions). Benchmarks engagement rate.
- **Conversions:** Key actions taken (email sign-ups, purchases, etc). Measures ROI.
- **CPM:** Cost per 1000 impressions. monitors ad spending

efficiency.

- **CPC:** Cost per click. Helps optimize bid amounts.
- **ROAS:** Return on ad spend. Critical for measuring overall value.

Analyze metrics daily and make ongoing optimizations to improve results. A/B test ad creative, offers, audiences and placements. Continually refine based on learnings.

Influencer Marketing Collaborations

Partnering with relevant influencers provides a major opportunity to expand your pet brand's reach and credibility. But successful influencer marketing requires careful strategy and execution.

Working with Other Influencers for Cross-Promotion

As a pet influencer, you likely already have relationships with other creators in your niche. Leverage these connections for collaborations that benefit both parties:

- Recruit influencers in complimentary pet niches (grooming, toys, food, vets, etc) for co-promotions.
- Trade shout-outs or guest posts to cross-leverage each other's audiences.
- Coordinate giveaways open to both audiences.
- Co-create content together centered around your pets.

Ensure collaborations feel authentic and add value for both audiences. Discuss potential partnerships thoroughly to align on expectations upfront.

Strategies for Successful Influencer Marketing

When recruiting influencers, consider reach, relevance, audience engagement and production quality. Check that their content and values align with your brand.

Some best practices for executing influencer campaigns:

- **Give creative freedom:** Let them showcase your brand authentically in their own style.
- **Promote broadly:** Have them post on all their social channels, email lists, etc.
- **Use creator codes:** Provide special offer codes for their audience.
- **Repurpose content:** Get rights to reuse their co-created content.
- **Measure actions:** Track clicks, conversions, etc. from their posts.

Make sure expectations, timelines, usage rights and performance metrics are defined in a detailed contractual agreement.

Measuring ROI on Influencer Campaigns

To assess campaign value, gather data on key performance indicators:

- **Audience reach:** How many new accounts did it expose your brand to?

- **Engagement:** Likes, comments and shares of their co-created posts.
- **Traffic:** Website visits and follows driven by the influencer.
- **Conversions:** Purchases, email sign-ups and other actions taken.
- **Earned media value:** What following the influencer provided in equivalent advertising spend.

Compare campaign expenses to the additional brand awareness, leads and sales generated to determine true ROI. Optimize based on findings.

Email Marketing and List Building

While social platforms are great for reach, email marketing enables more direct, personalized promotion to your engaged subscribers.

Creating Engaging Email Content

Use emails to build relationships with your subscribers. Tailor content to their interests:

- **Pet spotlights:** Profile adoptable pets from local shelters.
- **Pet care tips:** Share training, health and nutrition guidance.
- **Behind-the-scenes:** Give inside looks at your pets' daily lives.
- **Product updates:** Announce new merchandise or discounts.

- **Event notifications:** Promote meetups, adoption days, etc.
- **Pet influencer features:** Interview other popular pet accounts.

Keep copy concise, personable and scannable. Include eye-catching images and clear calls-to-action. Send from your pet's perspective for fun results.

Growing and Segmenting Email Lists

Offer lead magnets like discount codes and free guides in exchange for emails. Segment your list to send targeted content:

- **Geography:** Separate local vs. nationwide subscribers.
- **Interests:** Group based on pet types (dog, cat, etc) they want to see.
- **Engagement:** Filter highly engaged subscribers for VIP content.

Send segmented announcements, spotlights and discounts based on subscriber preferences for higher open and click rates.

Utilizing Email for Direct Marketing

While most of your email content should focus on relationship-building, you can also utilize your list for direct promotional purposes. Some ideas:

- **Product launches:** Give subscribers early access to new merchandise.
- **Special discounts:** Offer exclusive savings codes or flash sales.
- **Affiliate marketing:** Promote relevant partner brands and earn commissions.
- **Pre-order access:** Allow pre-orders of new products before general public release.

Time limited-time offers and product launches around peak engagement times for your list. Test subject lines and sending cadences to optimize open rates.

Final Thoughts: Advanced Social Media Marketing

Mastering paid advertising, influencer collaborations, and email marketing will take your pet influencer marketing to the next level. Remember to tailor messaging and offers to each audience, actively track performance metrics, and continually refine your efforts based on data and insights. With these advanced techniques, you can expand your reach, strengthen engagement, and build lasting connections with your ideal pet-loving community. The path to social media marketing mastery requires persistence, creativity and a little help from your furry friends!

FAQ

What are some best practices for Facebook ads for pet influencers?

Some best practices are interest-based targeting of pet lovers, creative that highlights your pets, relevant placements like Instagram feeds, and tracking engagement metrics like clicks and conversions. Test audiences, creatives and placements to optimize.

How much should I pay an influencer to feature my pet account?

Influencer fees vary greatly based on their reach and production quality. Smaller nano-influencers from $50-500, mid-tier from $500-$2000, and top-tier from $2000+. Make sure rates align with the value delivered through reach and engagement.

What type of content should I include in emails to subscribers?

Focus on providing value through pet care tips, cute pet spotlights, behind-the-scenes looks, product updates, local event promotions, and interviews with other pet influencers. Avoid overly promotional messaging.

How often should I email my list?

It depends on your open rates, but 1-2 times per week is fairly standard. Important to give subscribers valuable content without oversaturating their inboxes. Monitor engagement over time.

What are some ways to grow my email subscriber list?

Offer lead magnets in exchange for signups, promote signups on your social channels and website, collaborate with other influencers on co-promotions, and segment subscribers to send targeted content improving engagement.

25

Mental Health and Well-being in Pet Influencing

The world of pet influencing brings immense joy and fulfillment—but it can also take a toll on mental health. As creators, we pour our hearts into creating content, building a brand, and fostering community. But the demands of being an influencer, coupled with the complexities of life, can catalyze stress, anxiety, burnout, and other challenges. This chapter offers insights and strategies for protecting mental health amid the demands of pet influencing. By prioritizing wellness, seeking support, and promoting healthy messages, we can thrive in both life and work.

Addressing Stress and Anxiety

Juggling content creation, branding, sponsorships, and a personal life is no easy feat. The always-on nature of influencing can heighten stress and provoke anxiety. Left unaddressed, these issues can escalate and negatively impact mental health. But by recognizing signs of stress and intentionally managing it, influencers can mitigate these challenges.

Recognizing Signs of Stress in Pets and Owners

In order to manage stress, we must first recognize it. Signs of stress in pets may include:

- Excessive vocalization (barking, meowing)
- Aggression or changes in behavior
- Destructiveness (e.g. chewing items)
- House soiling
- Changes in appetite
- Lethargy/inactivity
- Excessive grooming behaviors

In humans, symptoms of stress and anxiety include:

- Changes in sleep patterns
- Low energy/fatigue
- Withdrawal from others
- Increased irritation/anger
- Poor concentration
- Changes in appetite
- Racing thoughts
- Muscle tension

Tuning into these warning signs helps us detect rising stress levels early when they are still manageable. This self-awareness empowers us to take action before anxiety escalates into a crisis.

Strategies for Managing Stress

Once we've pinpointed stress, we can employ strategies to dial it back down to healthy levels. Here are some science-backed techniques for easing anxiety:

Deep breathing - Taking slow, deep breaths signals our nervous system to relax. Try square breathing: inhale for 4 counts, hold for 4, exhale for 4, and pause for 4. Repeat for several minutes. Apps like Headspace offer guided breathing exercises.

Mindfulness meditation - Sitting quietly and focusing on the present moment reduces anxiety. Start with 5 minutes of mindfulness meditation using an app like Calm or Insight Timer.

Exercise - Working out releases endorphins which improve mood and relieve stress. Take your pet for a long walk, do yoga videos on YouTube, or exercise together by playing fetch.

Spending time in nature - Research shows being around plants and animals has a calming effect. Visit a park, garden, or hiking trail and unplug from technology. Bring your pet along too!

Talking to friends/family - Sharing feelings with loved ones alleviates isolation and builds emotional support. Vent your frustrations, ask for help, or simply enjoy quality time together.

Therapy - If anxiety persists, seeing a licensed mental health professional can provide targeted treatment. Many therapists now offer online video sessions.

The key is identifying go-to stress management strategies that work for you and making time to use them regularly, even amid the busyness of influencing.

Balancing Work and Personal Life

One significant source of stress stems from the blurred boundaries between personal and professional realms. Pet influencers often feel immense pressure to constantly create content, engage with followers, and network/collaborate with brands. Without reasonable limits, work easily encroaches on downtime and strains mental health.

Here are tips for better work-life balance:

- **Unplug regularly** - Set specific times each day/week to completely disconnect from work. For example, put away devices for family dinners or weekend mornings.
- **Set work hours** - Decide specific work hours and stick to them as much as possible. Communicate limited availability to followers.
- **Block off personal time** - Use calendars to schedule time off and reminders to take breaks. Honor this time as sacred.
- **Outsource tasks** - Consider hiring a social media assistant to handle administrative work like inbox management.
- **Practice self-care** - Prioritize healthy sleep, nutrition, exercise, social connection, and fun/relaxation.

With intention and boundaries, it's possible to keep work as a passion rather than burnout driver. Place mental health first—the content will still get created!

Maintaining Mental Health and Wellness

In the high-demand world of influencing, mental health maintenance is essential. From incorporating wellness practices into daily life to seeking professional support as needed, we must take a proactive approach to sustaining mental health amid stressors.

Mindfulness and Mental Health Practices

Carving out time for centering, restorative activities bolsters the mind and emotions. Consider weaving these practices into your regular routine:

- **Morning pages** - Journal stream-of-consciousness without editing for 10 minutes upon waking.
- **Guided visualization** - Use apps to do relaxing guided imagery for mental escape and focus.
- **Gratitude journaling** - Jot down 3-5 things you're grateful for daily. Boosts positivity.
- **Relaxation exercises** - Do body scans, progressive muscle relaxation, and visualization.
- **Breathwork** - Spend 5-10 minutes focusing solely on your breath.
- **Mindful walking** - Take mindful strolls periodically throughout your day.
- **Digital detox** - Initiate 30-60 min tech breaks where you set aside devices.
- **Nature immersion** - Spend time walking, sitting, or playing with your pet outside.

283

Weaving brief mental health mini-practices throughout your day cultivates resilience when stressors arise. Start small with 5-minute exercises and gradually increase frequency and duration. Think preventatively.

Seeking Support and Professional Help

Despite best efforts at self-care, serious mental health issues can still emerge. Warning signs include:

- Apathy/lack of interest in normal activities
- Extreme changes in sleep, appetite, mood
- Inability to focus or make decisions
- Thoughts of self-harm

Should these or other concerning symptoms appear, seeking professional help promptly is critical—this is not something you have to tackle alone. Some options to consider:

- **Therapy** - Psychologists, counselors, and therapists provide strategies for improving mental health. Search sites like Psychology Today to find practitioners.
- **Psychiatrist** - Psychiatrists can prescribe medications to help stabilize mood or anxiety in conjunction with therapy. Ask your primary care provider for referrals.
- **Support groups** - Group meetings for conditions like depression or grief provide community aid. NAMI lists options.
- **Emergency resources** - If you or someone you know is at immediate risk, call emergency services or the National Suicide Prevention Lifeline at 988.

Seeking help takes courage, but equips us with needed care. Our mental health deserves the same care we give to our pets and followers.

Fostering a Healthy Online Environment

The cyberworld of influencing brings unique stressors. From managing community expectations to weathering hateful comments, the virtual space can tax mental health. Setting compassionate but firm boundaries bolsters well-being.

- **Moderate comments** - Don't tolerate trolls or bullies. Delete/block them immediately to prevent escalation.
- **Set online hours** - Clearly communicate when you will be engaged online versus off-the-grid. Stick to defined times.
- **Limit notifications** - Mute non-essential apps and disable push notifications to reduce digital overload.
- **Model positive behaviors** - Demonstrate healthy limits and self-care practices online. Inspire your community to do the same.

The online space is our office. By keeping it a mentally healthy environment, we can prevent it from becoming a source of harm.

Promoting Positive Mental Health Messages

As influencers, we have a platform to spread awareness and advocate for mental health—not just our own, but also our audience's. By normalizing open dialogue, sharing stories, and offering encouragement, we create ripple effects of support.

Advocating for Mental Health Awareness

Use your platform to advocate for improved societal understanding of mental health. Help dispel myths and break stigmas by openly discussing facts. For example:

- **Share statistics** - "1 in 5 adults experience mental illness each year. Help is available."
- **Promote resources** - "If you're struggling, call the Substance Abuse and Mental Health Services Administration's free helpline: 1-800-662-HELP (4357). Trained counselors are available 24/7."
- **Encourage compassion** - "Be extra kind today—you don't know what silent battles someone may be fighting."

Just incorporating simple messages of hope makes a difference. Follow and share organizations dedicated to mental health education like MHA and Bring Change 2 Mind. Together we can normalize mental health as part of overall health.

Sharing Personal Experiences and Stories

Our own stories of struggling with and overcoming mental health challenges reassure others they aren't alone. Consider opening up about your mental health journey when you feel comfortable:

- Share experiences getting help for issues like depression, anxiety, OCD, PTSD, etc.
- Discuss mental health stigma you've encountered and how you push past it.
- Get vulnerable about times you've struggled and what got you through.
- Offer tips that have worked for improving your own mental health.

Your courage to share inspires others to open up and seek help too. Through community and connection, we heal.

Encouraging Open Dialogue on Mental Health

Creating open, non-judgmental spaces for discussing mental health fosters support and understanding. Ways to encourage healthy dialogue include:

- Sharing facts/statistics about mental health.
- Destigmatizing therapy and medication.
- Validating others' feelings and experiences without minimizing them.
- Asking thoughtful questions about how people are authentically doing.
- Allowing silences and not forcing/rushing vulnerable conversations.
- Providing encouragement and positive feedback when people share struggles.
- Recommending professional resources if concerns arise about someone's mental state.
- Checking in regularly with your community and remind-

ing them you care.

With compassion and wisdom, we can create online sanctuaries where people feel safe confiding their mental health experiences without shame or judgment. Our platforms become communities of care.

Final Thoughts on Influencer Mental Health

The demands of influencing coupled with simply being human mean mental health requires ongoing care. But by honoring our limits, embracing support, and promoting healthy messages, we can balance fulfilling careers with emotional well-being. Our pets, fans and we ourselves deserve nothing less. Stay true to your heart—it's your most precious asset.

Frequently Asked Questions About Influencer Mental Health

How can I tell if my mental health is declining?

- Watch for emotional symptoms like increased anxiety/sadness, isolation, irritability, lack of motivation.
- Monitor physical signs such as changes in appetite, sleep patterns, energy levels.
- Pay attention if responsibilities become difficult to manage.
- Take note if you lose interest in activities normally enjoyed.

What should I do if I'm feeling depressed or suicidal?

- First and foremost, seek immediate emergency care by calling 911, visiting an ER, or contacting the National Suicide Prevention Lifeline at 988. You deserve help.
- Make an appointment with a mental health professional like a psychologist or psychiatrist. Ask your doctor for referrals.
- Confide in trusted friends/family and request support.
- Remove anything in your home you could use to harm yourself.
- List reasons to live and read them whenever suicidal thoughts occur.

How can I help a friend struggling with their mental health?

- Listen attentively without judgment if they confide issues. Validate their feelings.
- Offer to research professional help options and accompany them to appointments.
- Check in regularly via text/call to remind them you care. But respect any requests for space.
- Suggest healthy self-care activities you can do together like taking a walk or cooking a meal.
- Recommend the emergency help lines if you feel they are in immediate danger of self-harm.

What are signs my pet may be stressed?

Potential indicators of stress in pets include: excessive vocalizing or barking, aggressive behavior, destructive chewing/scratching, house soiling, changes in appetite, lethargy, anxiety, and excessive grooming or fur loss. Pay attention to any behavioral shifts.

How can I find an affordable therapist?

- Check with your health insurance to see which mental health providers are covered.
- Search online directories like Psychology Today and filter by insurance.
- Investigate low-cost community mental health clinics.
- Ask if therapists offer discounted rates for financial hardship. Many will work with you.
- Consider online video therapy which expands access to affordable providers.

26

Sustainability in Pet Influencing

Eco-Friendly Practices and Products

As the pet influencing space continues to grow, there is increasing awareness around the environmental impact of popular pet products and practices. More pet owners are seeking out sustainable options, and influencers have a unique opportunity to promote eco-friendly brands and habits to their audiences.

Promoting Sustainable Pet Products

One way pet influencers can integrate sustainability is by featuring and recommending eco-conscious pet products. There are now many brands creating innovative solutions for reducing waste in the pet industry.

For example, subscription services like **BarkBox** and **Pup-Box** now offer recyclable toy options made from natural materials like rubber and cotton. Pet food companies like **The**

Honest Kitchen utilize compostable packaging and ethically sourced ingredients. Even litter and waste bags are getting a sustainable makeover from brands like **BioBag** that offer plant-based and biodegradable options.

By partnering with and promoting these purpose-driven companies, influencers can provide their followers with easy, eco-friendly swaps for daily pet essentials. Small changes like these can have an outsized impact, especially when adopted by the large audiences many pet influencers have cultivated.

An influencer doesn't necessarily have to overhaul their partnerships or content calendar to incorporate sustainability. Simple tips like "here are my top 5 sustainable pet products" or "check out these eco-friendly ideas" can gently introduce the concept to their community.

Implementing Green Practices

In addition to curating green products, pet influencers can adopt sustainable practices in their own lives and content creation. With behind-the-scenes peeks into their daily routines, influencers have the power to inspire lifestyle changes that benefit the environment.

For example, emphasizing reusable products over disposable plastic is an easy switch. Stainless steel bowls, wood chew toys, and glass food containers are attractive, long-lasting options. Packing treats and meals in reusable snack bags and containers reduces waste. Even keeping a stash of old towels and blankets for messes and accidents prevents paper towel overuse.

Other small habit changes like providing pet-safe plants for enrichment, composting pet waste, and saving water during bath time are simple but significant. Providing tips on proper disposal of medications, toxic waste, and electronics prevents contaminants entering landfills and waterways.

When creating content, pet influencers can opt for sustainable props and backdrops. Sourcing antlers, sticks, and other natural materials from ethical vendors avoids unethical harvesting. Filming primarily in natural outdoor settings reduces studio resources and energy. Renting items or sourcing from secondhand shops lowers consumption. Details like these demonstrate an eco-conscious mindset.

Raising Awareness on Environmental Impact

As leaders in the pet space, influencers have a responsibility beyond promoting products and deals. Pet ownership has exploded in popularity, and improper education around issues like overbreeding, exotic pet trade, and environmental impact has led to negative consequences. However, influencers have the platform and trust to course-correct and provide better guidance.

One great example is raising awareness around proper wildlife interactions. Images of exotic animals as pets or questionable human-animal encounters often go viral for entertainment. However, mistreatment and habitat destruction enables this exploitation, even if indirectly, when promoted noncritically.

Influencers can thoughtfully examine the ethics and sustainability of their partnerships and content. Vocalizing concern over shark finning, elephant rides, and other exploitative tourism redirects the conversation to conservation. Likewise, speaking out against puppy mills and irresponsible breeding centers attention on adoption and population control.

Sustainability also extends to physical habitats. Pet enrich-ment advice cautioning against harmful foraging prevents de-forestation. Discouraging outdoor cats helps protect wildlife populations and ecosystems. Even simple location tags educate followers on fragility of natural sites. Ultimately, the pet community has the power to preserve our environment simply by promoting compassion for all creatures.

Supporting Conservation Efforts

Pet influencers are passionate about animals by nature. Thus, championing wildlife and environmental conservation aligns seamlessly with their brands. Dedicating resources to these worthy causes creates positive change.

Collaborating with Conservation Organizations

One major way to contribute is teaming up directly with impactful nonprofit organizations. For example, animal welfare groups like the ASPCA and HSUS work tirelessly to end animal cruelty and exploitation. Their lobbying, education, and rescue initiatives benefit tremendously from expanded awareness.

Likewise, conservation nonprofits like the World Wildlife Fund (WWF) and Oceana protect at-risk species and threat-ened ecosystems. They aim to address issues like climate change, deforestation, and ocean pollution that threaten biodiversity and natural habitats. Their outreach and policy work preserve beautiful but fragile environments.

Donating proceeds from merchandise or sponsored content

provides these groups with funding to continue their efforts. Featuring adoptable shelter pets boosts adoption numbers and saves lives. Fundraising campaigns activate follower networks on important issues. Even posting informative infographics and statistics from these organizations expands critical education.

Promoting donation drives like pet food, blankets and toys for shelter pets or coral reef restoration projects engages audiences as well. Visiting facilities to provide exposure through exclusive content conveys the meaningful results conservation nonprofits achieve. Ultimately, pet influencers have the platform and credibility to provide vital amplification for their messages.

Educational Campaigns on Wildlife and Habitat

In addition to signal-boosting larger NGOs, pet influencers can launch their own philanthropic campaigns centered on wildlife and environmental education. The engaging storytelling and emotional connections they build with followers can inspire impactful change.

For example, an educational series on endangered species helps showcase amazing biodiversity. Facts on dwindling populations and success stories of species like pandas, whales, and cheetahs inspire support. Examining the pet trade's damage on populations through poaching and smuggling highlights important welfare issues.

Likewise, an ocean conservation initiative brings awareness to pollution, overfishing and climate impacts on delicate marine ecosystems. Marine species profiles and small habit adjustments that improve coastal health provide tangible steps to get involved.

Even hyperlocal projects in one's own community create change. Clean-up drives remove waste from beaches and parks. Planting projects restore wildlife habitats. Surveying local wildlife populations tracks biodiversity. These small, hands-on campaigns empower ordinary citizens to become more engaged stewards of the planet.

Encouraging Community Involvement in Conservation

To build on educational content, influencers can provide clear calls-to-action that mobilize followers to engage in conservation efforts themselves. The supportive communities that influencers foster are eager for ways to contribute.

For example, promoting animal foster programs gives followers a direct way to aid shelter rehabilitation efforts through hands-on volunteering. Participating in petition drives and fundraising campaigns activates their network to advocate for legislative protections.

Spotlighting local conservation groups and volunteer opportunities connects followers to impactful projects. Simple tips like litter clean-up while walking dogs or contacting representatives on key environmental bills facilitate genuinely helpful participation.

Even creative initiatives like social media contests and hashtags expand engagement. Competitions for volunteer hours logged or trash collected gamify participation. Sustainability challenges encourage followers to gradually improve habits. Ultimately, the diverse, loyal audience influencers command can drive real impact across causes when mobilized collectively.

Reducing Carbon Footprint

As public figures for the pet community, influencers must also assess their own environmental footprint associated with content creation and business operations. Committing to meaningful offsets and sustainable practices demonstrates accountability.

Minimizing Travel and Energy Use

Influencer work inevitably involves transportation through commuting, errands, events and content production. Accordingly, reducing car and air travel slashes an individual's carbon footprint significantly.

Ridesharing, biking and public transport opt for lower-emission options over personal vehicles. Combining errands and shopping trips into one outing conserves gas. Choosing central locations close to home for content creation minimizes drive times. For necessary air travel, investing in high-quality carbon offsets helps address impact.

At-home energy conservation offers additional reductions. Using natural light and efficient lightbulbs cuts electricity usage. Unplugging devices, activating sleep settings, and upgrading to EnergyStar appliances also help. Simple acts like line-drying, adjusting thermostats and reducing water waste during bathing provide tiny but tangible improvements.

Sustainable Packaging and Shipping

Pet influencers and brands frequently send mailers, swag bags and orders requiring packaging and shipping. Sourcing sustainable materials like recycled paper or plant-based bioplastics reduces associated waste.

Minimizing packaging also helps; eliminating excess filler, avoiding oversized boxes, and foregoing unnecessary outer packaging cuts down on materials. Electronic delivery replaces physical shipments whenever possible.

Choosing low-emission carriers like USPS over air freight also lowers the transport footprint. Local sourcing and manufacturing prevents freight from racking up excessive overland miles as well. Taking inventory of vendors' sustainability practices ensures an eco-conscious supply chain.

Carbon Offsetting and Green Initiatives

To address unavoidable emissions, direct carbon offsetting effectively counterbalances environmental impact. Purchasing credits through vetted organizations like Terrapass, Bonneville Environmental Foundation (BEF) and Cool Effect funds initiatives that actively remove carbon and combat climate change.

Influencers can also launch their own green projects to offset operational footprint. Starting community gardens, planting trees, restoring wetlands and donating solar panels offer hands-on initiatives that benefit the environment and local community.

Installing smart systems like programmable thermostats, rainwater collection barrels, solar panels and EV charging stations green one's personal home or office spaces as well. Efficiency upgrades to lighting, insulation and appliances optimize business facilities over time. Dedicating workspace sections to live plants improves indoor air quality too.

Ultimately, sustainability requires evaluating impact holistically across products, practices and spaces. With consciousness and accountability, the collective pet community can preserve the planet we cherish. Our furry friends depend on it.

Frequently Asked Questions on Sustainability and Pet Influencing

How can pet influencers promote sustainability?

Pet influencers can promote sustainability by partnering with eco-friendly brands, implementing green practices in their own lives, raising awareness on conservation issues, supporting environmental nonprofits, and reducing their own carbon footprint through offsets and efficiency upgrades. Small changes make a big difference when scaled to their large audiences.

What are some examples of sustainable pet products?

Examples of sustainable pet products include recyclable/-compostable toys and treats packaging, ethically sourced and natural ingredients in foods and grooming products, reusable accessories like bowls and poop bag holders, cleaning concentrates that reduce plastic waste, and earth-friendly waste disposal solutions like compostable litter or bags.

What green practices can pet owners adopt?

Green practices pet owners can adopt include utilizing reusable accessories, choosing natural and recycled materials for bedding/toys, providing plant-based enrichment, composting pet waste, conserving water, properly disposing of hazardous waste, shopping secondhand and local, and opting for sustainable transportation.

How does pet ownership impact the environment?

Pet ownership strains the environment through factors like production of meat-based kibble, manufacturing of plastics/packaging, emissions from transportation, improper waste disposal, use of toxic grooming chemicals, and damage to wildlife populations from free-roaming pets. However, pet influencers can provide education on reducing these impacts.

Why is sustainability important for pet influencers?

Sustainability is important for pet influencers because they have large platforms that impact many followers, significant production footprints from content creation and shipping, and a responsibility as animal lovers to protect habitats and species. Leading by example allows the community to collectively benefit the planet.

27

Creating a Signature Style for Your Pet Brand

Defining Your Brand Aesthetics

Creating a strong visual identity is crucial for standing out in the crowded world of pet influencers. Your brand's aesthetics—including color palette, fonts, imagery style, and more—allow followers to recognize your content instantly. Defining and sticking to signature design elements across platforms creates consistency and amplifies your brand authority.

Establishing a Unique Visual Identity

The first step is pinpointing the feel you want to evoke with your branding. Are you bold and funky or classic and refined? Urban hipster or rugged outdoorsy? Your brand character should align with your pet's personality and your target audience.

Once you've settled on an overarching aesthetic, establish 2-3 primary color tones that will define your look across channels. Instagram grids with a cohesive color story have high visual impact.

Choose creative fonts that express your vibe, using free font websites if needed. Handwritten or display fonts with personality work for pet brands. Stick to 2 main fonts—one for headlines and one for body text. Being consistent makes you memorable.

Develop original graphic elements like patterns, borders, illustrations that can unify your branding. A custom avatar featuring your pet is a smart investment for instant recognition. Watermarks work well on images to solidify your brand.

Crafting a Consistent Look and Feel

Achieving a consistent branding style demonstrates professionalism and authority. Using templates with your defined design elements for images, posts, highlights reels, and more makes content creation easier while keeping your aesthetic on-point.

Photos should have a signature look regarding lighting, angle, composition, editing style, and other photographic choices. Videos should incorporate intro/outro slides, graphics, and music that match your brand vibe.

Even small details like social media icons, website layout, email newsletter design, and merch should all coordinate, so followers encounter familiar visuals. Repetition strengthens recognition.

Branding Across Different Platforms

Optimizing branding for each platform's specifications is key for making your content stand out.

For Instagram, use all available real estate. Maximize image sizes, fill bio with keywords, utilize highlights and story templates.

YouTube allows channel art, thumbnails, branding watermarks, end screens, and more customization.

Leverage Pinterest sections, TikTok sticker fonts and effects, Twitter brand highlights. Configure platforms to showcase your signature look.

Cross-promote new content across your socials consistently. Multi-channel reinforcement amplifies authority through repetition of visual branding.

Innovating with Design and Creativity

A strategic brand identity remains effective over the long-term. However, incorporating new creative elements keeps your content fresh and engaging. Pushing aesthetic boundaries demonstrates your originality as an influencer.

Experimenting with Visual Styles

Trying Instagram themes like color gradients, geometric frames, or grunge effects allows you to gauge follower response. Change up photographic editing styles to create enticing before-and-after comparisons.

Spice up static posts with animated text, illustrations, or graphic accents using apps like Canva. Overlays and textures lend visual interest to images.

Explore different shooting locations in natural light, at golden hour, sunsets, with lens flares. Use props and backgrounds that inspire you artistically.

Creative Branding Techniques

Innovative branding elevates your identity beyond the expected. Custom illustrations and graphic design elements incorporated into templates and merch give a premium, bespoke feel.

Embrace humor and get playful with quirky fonts, irreverent graphics, or meme-style images. This humanizes your brand for Millennial/Gen Z audiences.

Try unconventional photography like aerial shots by drone, epic action sequences, minimalist composition, or moody lighting. Edgy imagery performs well.

Keeping Your Brand Fresh and Relevant

While consistency shapes recognition, evolving aesthetics keeps you relevant as trends change. Monitor branding of influencers you admire and list competitors to avoid overlap.

Know when to retire overused elements that risk looking dated. Introduce new colors, graphic motifs, layouts, and photography approaches incrementally.

Infuse novelty through collaborations with other pet brands for guest posts, influencer events or joint products. Co-branding initiatives stimulate creativity.

Integrating Style with Substance

Ultimately, strong branding should elevate your content rather than act as a superficial substitute. When visual presentation harmonizes with substance, you amplify engagement and trust.

Ensuring Visuals Match Brand Values

Your aesthetic choices should authentically reflect your brand's core focus and values. For example, an eco-friendly pet care brand may opt for natural tones, hand-drawn fonts and illustrated imagery to align with their mission.

Photos of pets enjoying your products/services in the appropriate context reinforce what your brand offers. Supportive visuals boost believability.

Infographics, charts and graphics help simplify complex topics for readers, making information more digestible when paired with stylish visuals.

Balancing Style with Content Quality

Great branding can help mediocre content get initial attention, but it becomes meaningless without valuable information.

Focus first on developing high-quality content that solves your audience's needs. Then enhance it with aesthetics that reflect your brand identity. Substance takes priority.

Use visuals sparingly to avoid cognitive overload. Too many competing fonts, graphics, animations distract from your message.

Storytelling Through Design

Thoughtful design choices can add layers of meaning to elevate dry topics. Color psychology taps into emotional responses—blue tones are calming while reds grab attention.

Repeated visual motifs create cohesion in long-form tutorials or training guides, guiding the reader's focus across sections.

Illustrations and custom photography in blog posts or social graphics enable you to show rather than tell for powerful storytelling.

Final Thoughts: Creating a Signature Style for Your Pet Brand

Defining consistent, recognizable aesthetics allows you to cut through the noise in the crowded pet influencer space. However, integrating innovative accents keeps your visual voice fresh, engaging and forward-thinking. Most importantly, ensure your branding authentically communicates your brand values visually for maximum trust and connection with your loyal followers.

FAQs About Creating a Signature Style for Your Pet Brand

What are some examples of strong aesthetic branding in the pet influencer industry?

Some examples of pet influencers with distinctive visual branding include The Dogist's black-and-white portrait photography, Dog With a Blog's use of colorful backgrounds and props, and The Kitty's hand-drawn illustrations and fonts.

How often should I update my brand's overall aesthetic?

You should aim to refresh your overall visual branding every 2-3 years to stay fresh. However, you can introduce minor styling updates more frequently to keep things evolving.

What's better for branding: consistency or creativity?

Ideally, you want to blend both consistency, through recurring visual elements like color schemes and fonts, with spurts of creativity via new graphic accents, animations, photography styles. Consistency builds recognition, while creativity keeps things exciting.

What are some easy ways to create branded social media templates?

Apps like Canva, Adobe Spark, and InShot make it simple to design branded templates with custom fonts, colors, and graphics that you can reuse across platforms.

How can I make sure my branding doesn't appear outdated?

Stay on top of current design trends via sites like Dribbble. Look at competitor branding and note elements that feel fresh. Solicit objective feedback from followers on your aesthetic and upgrade accordingly.

28

Data-Driven Strategies for Pet Influencers

In the world of influencer marketing, data is king. For pet influencers looking to grow and monetize their online presence, leveraging data-driven strategies can provide a key competitive advantage. From optimizing content to enhancing social media profiles, analytics empower influencers to make smarter decisions that directly impact their success.

Leveraging Data for Content Strategy

Crafting content that resonates with your target audience is critical for pet influencers. The days of guessing what followers might enjoy are over. Now, concrete data provides valuable insights to directly inform content creation and maximize engagement.

Analyzing Audience Insights

Social media platforms provide detailed analytics into your followers and their interests. Studying these insights allows you to craft content tailored specifically for your community.

For example, you can view demographic data like age, gender, location, language, and active hours. This reveals your target audience's attributes. Knowing that 80% of your Instagram followers are 18-35 year old females in the United States tells you quite a bit about their potential interests and preferences.

You can also analyze audience engagement metrics on existing content. Look at your top performing posts over the last 3-6 months. What type of content gets the most likes, comments, and shares? The common themes and characteristics reveal what resonates best with your followers.

And don't just look at your own account. Study competitors and industry leaders in your niche to identify broader content trends and opportunities. What are other popular pet influencers creating that engages their audiences? The data holds the answers.

Content Performance Metrics

Measure the performance of your content across multiple factors:

- **Impressions** - how many times your content is displayed
- **Reach** - the number of unique accounts that see it
- **Engagement rate** - how much interaction it drives from followers

- **Comments** - what people are saying about your posts
- **Shares** - how often content is being reshared
- **Saves** - how many times people bookmark your content
- **Link clicks** - how many users click links in your posts
- **Hashtag performance** - how well chosen hashtags res-onate

Analyze these metrics over time to identify your best and worst performing content. Then double down on what works and adjust what doesn't. The data reveals content gaps and opportunities.

For example, a sponsored post around Christmas may drive lots of impressions and reach. But if the engagement rate is low, you know it failed to truly resonate despite the extra visibility.

Or perhaps posts themed around cute puppies perform better than educational tips. You can tailor future content to focus more on viral, emotional hooks while still incorporating advice.

Predictive Analysis for Future Trends

Leverage historical performance data to predict future out-comes. Platforms like Facebook and Instagram provide predictive analysis tools to estimate how new posts might perform even before you publish them.

Review factors like past engagement rates on posts with similar content, follower feedback, likes, and current trends. Then use these predictions to plan out an editorial calendar that aligns with audience interests.

Scheduling content that is statistically more likely to do

well increases the odds of driving engagement and growth. While surprises can always happen, avoiding dud posts by using data insights helps raise overall performance.

Optimizing Social Media Profiles

Your social media profiles represent a virtual storefront - optimized design and branding attract more visitors. Analytics tools empower pet influencers to A/B test profile elements and improve the user experience.

Profile Optimization Techniques

Start by setting specific profile optimization goals based on target metrics:

- Increase profile views by 25%
- Boost clicks on website link in bio by 50%
- Grow follower count 15% month-over-month

Then use data to identify optimization opportunities. Testing profile elements like usernames, profile pictures, bios, keywords, visual branding, links, and more allows you to measure direct impact on goals.

For example, consider changing your Instagram handle from @brunosadventures to @brunothesausagepuppy. Use analytics to monitor profile views for 2 weeks before and after the change. The data reveals whether this attracts more visitors by clarifying your pet niche focus.

A/B Testing for Profile Elements

Run A/B tests by making a small change to your profile for a set period while keeping the rest the same. Then switch back and compare metrics.

Some elements that can be A/B tested include:

- Profile picture
- Bio description
- External links
- Profile name
- Captions
- Visual branding like color schemes

The key is to only change one variable at a time. This isolates the impact of your test change.

For example, you can test whether a cute photo or professional headshot works better as a profile picture for driving follower growth. Try the cute photo for 1 week, then switch to the headshot for 1 week. The data clearly shows which resulted in more followers.

Using Data to Improve User Experience

Profile analytics also provide insight into your followers' interests, pain points, and goals. Visitor demographics, interactions, clicks, and feedback help you understand user behavior.

Then improve experience by tailoring profiles to your audience. For example, if 50% of visitors click your Petco affiliate link, they likely want deals on pet products. Make sure this link stands out.

Data reveals new opportunities. Follower questions and feedback indicate gaps in your content. Click flow patterns show navigation issues. Measure and optimize to create profiles that followers love interacting with.

Data Privacy and Ethical Considerations

While data delivers a wealth of insights, pet influencers must also use analytics in an ethical manner that respects user privacy. Following ever-evolving regulations is key.

Understanding Data Privacy Laws

Be aware of major data privacy laws like the EU's GDPR and California's CCPA. These protect user data and regulate how it can be legally collected and leveraged.

Key requirements include:

- Explicit opt-in consent to gather data
- Notifying users how data will be used
- Allowing users to access/delete their data
- Implementing data security measures
- Limited retention periods for data storage
- Privacy policy explaining practices

Fines for violations can be massive. Stay updated on changes to ensure compliance. Using analytics ethically builds audience trust.

Ethical Use of Data in Marketing

Never implement tactics meant solely to manipulate followers or promote questionable products. While the data may show an approach drives clicks, unethical practices ultimately harm your brand.

Avoid leveraging data to:

- Promote products known for animal cruelty
- Target vulnerable groups with misinformation
- Use psychographic profiling in manipulative ways
- Violate user privacy expectations
- Spread dangerous or false content, even if it performs well

The ends do not justify the means. More followers or sales generated unethically never outweigh potential damage to reputation and trust. Use data to delight users, not deceive them.

Transparency is key - notify your audience about how you leverage analytics. Seek direct consent where applicable. And offer ways to opt-out of data collection.

Prioritizing ethics earns audience respect. And in the long run, reputation drives growth more than gimmicks.

Final Thoughts: Data-Driven Strategies for Pet Influencers

Data provides a roadmap to help pet influencers thrive in a competitive market. But analytics should be viewed as a guide, not a rigid rulebook. Creativity and authenticity still reign supreme - data only aims to sharpen the human edge.

Leverage insights to optimize, but let passion craft content. Use metrics to increase efficiency, but maintain your unique voice. And implement data-driven strategies only within an ethical framework of transparency.

In the end, the human relationships you build with your pet loving community are the true force that propels success. Data simply lights the way. By embracing analytics while championing creativity, pet influencers can nurture authentic engagement that turns followers into lifelong brand evangelists.

FAQs: Data-Driven Strategies for Pet Influencers

What are some key metrics pet influencers should track?

Some of the most important metrics to track include: engagement rate, link clicks, impressions, reach, hashtag performance, audience demographics, and content comments. Monitoring these factors helps optimize content strategy and social media profiles.

How can I A/B test elements of my Instagram profile?

Run A/B tests by changing one variable on your profile for a set period, such as 1-2 weeks, then switching back to compare impact on metrics. Test profile photo, description, name, external links, captions, color schemes, and other elements. Keep the rest of your profile unchanged to isolate impact.

What are some ethical ways to use data in my influencer marketing?

Use data transparently to create content and experiences tailored for your audience. Seek direct consent where applicable. Avoid manipulative or deceptive tactics just to drive growth. Never promote unethical or dangerous products/claims solely because data shows they perform well. Prioritize audience trust.

Why is analyzing my competitor's social media metrics useful?

Studying what performs well for competitors reveals broader trends and opportunities in your niche. Identify types of content that tend to get high engagement amongst the pet influencer community. Then create your own versions optimized for your audience.

How can I legally leverage analytics while respecting user privacy?

Understand major privacy laws like GDPR and CCPA. Follow requirements for data consent, security, storage, and transparency. Notify users how you utilize data. Provide opt-out options. Update practices to comply with changing regulations. Follow guidelines, and data will strengthen trust.

29

Cultivating Community Engagement and Interaction

In the world of pet influencers, building an engaged community around your furry friend is critical for gaining and maintaining followers. But simply posting cute photos is not enough to create lasting, meaningful connections. Savvy pet influencers must go beyond the fluff and deliberately cultivate interactive, supportive communities both on and offline.

Creating Interactive and Engaging Content

Gone are the days where pet influencers could gain a massive following from simply posting adorable pet photos. With over 471 million pet influencer posts in 2021 alone, standing out takes creativity and thinking beyond just cute animal content. By designing your content strategy to encourage audience participation, you make your community feel valued and involved, leading to higher engagement rates and loyal followers.

Designing Content for Audience Participation

The key to good engagement starts with crafting content with your audience in mind. How can you encourage your followers to not just view your posts, but actively participate?

- **Ask questions:** Pose questions directly to your audience related to the topic, then respond to comments. This content performs well as it prompts discussion.
- **Run polls:** Instagram Polls, Twitter Polls, and other interactive polls keep followers engaged. Poll about favorite products, names for a new pet, or where to donate.
- **Host contests/giveaways:** Follower contests drive comments, shares, and tags. Require followers to tag friends, answer a question, or share a post to enter.
- **Share user-generated content:** Reposting and crediting user photos or videos of your pet makes followers feel special.
- **Go live:** Livestreams allow real-time interaction and audience participation. Read comments aloud and respond in real-time.
- **Be responsive:** Reply to comments, answer questions, and thank new followers. This genuine interaction goes a long way.
- **Share behind-the-scenes:** Give followers a peek behind the cutesy photos into your real life. They'll relate to the silly outtakes and bloopers.
- **Encourage UGC:** Explicitly invite audience content submissions like fan art or pet parodies of your photos. Reposting this UGC delights followers.

Keep these tactics in mind when planning content. Unique, interactive content earns more engagement and helps form community connections.

Hosting Q&A Sessions and AMAs

Hosting live or written Q&A sessions is hugely popular, allowing followers to get their pressing questions answered.

For live Q&As, broadcast on platforms like Instagram or YouTube. Monitor comments and respond verbally in real time.

For written Q&As, open it up on your feed or stories. Ask followers to submit questions, then post a series of responses.

Q&As allow you to share insider information followers crave. It also enables you to get to know your audience better through the types of questions asked.

Consider regularly scheduling monthly or quarterly Q&As to give fans an open forum. Promote the Q&A schedule on your channels to build anticipation.

To source great questions, allow followers to submit questions in advance. Curate and group questions by theme for an organized, easy-to-follow session.

If going live feels intimidating as a new pet influencer, start by recording Q&As to post later. This allows editing freedom without the pressures of live interaction.

Mix up written and video Q&As to appeal to different audiences. Written Q&As also enable optimizing responses for SEO by including relevant keywords.

Encouraging User-Generated Content

User-generated content (UGC) is any form of content created by your followers and fans. This includes photos, videos, reviews, testimonials, fan art, and more.

UGC provides free, authentic content you can share while showing off your engaged community. It also gives fans a creative outlet to showcase their love for your pet.

Some ways to encourage UGC include:

- **Photo challenges:** Give followers photo prompts or challenges to create specific images. For example, submit photos of pets accessorized in a certain color.
- **Spotlighting fan art:** Ask followers to submit fan art or other creative works featuring your pet. Repost standouts.
- **Sharing testimonials:** Request video or written testimonials about your pet, brand, or content, then share them.
- **Pet parodies:** Invite fans to create fun pet parody photos or videos mimicking your content's style. These tend to go viral.
- **Product reviews:** Ask your community to post reviews of pet products you recommend. Share the most helpful.
- **Hashtag campaigns:** Launch hashtag campaigns where users submit UGC around a central theme like #TongueOutTuesday. The results can be compiled into user collections on your profile.

When resharing UGC, always credit the original creator and link to their profile. UGC provides a win-win - you gain fresh content while fans get recognition. Maintaining this cycle of engagement keeps community members invested in your long-term success.

Building a Strong Online Community

Simply gaining new followers is not enough. To succeed long term, pet influencers must build communities where members are invested and engaged over an extended time period. This level of community requires effort but pays dividends down the road through higher engagement rates, referrals, and sales conversions.

Nurturing a Supportive and Active Community

You want your community to be a friendly place where people support each other around a shared love for your pet. Some ways to cultivate this type of positive environment include:

- **Set community rules/guidelines:** Communicate the type of community you want to build through published rules of respect, constructive dialog, and inclusiveness.
- **Moderate when needed:** Keep discussions on track by filtering harmful comments and maintaining a constructive tone.
- **Lead by example:** Demonstrate the supportive, kind tone you wish to see via your own comments and interactions.
- **Give back:** Support animal welfare causes and encourage followers to do the same through fundraisers or volunteer options.
- ** Foster connections:** Host regular live chats or groups where community members can interact in real

time.

- **Highlight superfans:** Create a "Pet of the Week" or "Fan Spotlight" to recognize especially engaged members.
- **Encourage sharing:** Urge members to share your pet with friends to grow the community. Make it easy by providing sample posts or emails for them to pass along.

Taking a hands-on role in shaping the community creates a welcoming hub where friendships and connections blossom between members well beyond just being shared followers of your pet.

Strategies for Community Growth

Growing your pet community takes time, consistency, and smart strategies beyond just creating great content. Some proven ways to expand your community include:

- **Cross-promote across platforms:** Link between your Instagram, YouTube, TikTok, Twitter to drive followers from one platform to another.
- **Run contests/giveaways:** Follower contests that encourage shares and tags can rapidly expand your audience. Require contest entries on multiple platforms to maximize reach.
- **Collaborate with other pet influencers:** Coordinate co-hosting livestreams or swapping takeovers to tap into each other's audiences.
- **Hashtag campaigns:** Create unique hashtags related to your pet or brand that followers can rally around and share out to their own networks. Track performance with

hashtag analytics.

- **Interact with followers of similar accounts:** Take time to engage with followers of other pet influencers in your niche by commenting and liking their content. Some will check you out and follow.
- **Comment on influencer posts:** Leaving thoughtful comments on posts from more prominent pet influencers can lead to follows, especially if they reply back.
- **Guest post:** Contribute guest posts or videos for other pet sites and influencers. Include links back to your website or social profiles.
- **Run paid ads:** Use highly targeted paid ads on platforms like Facebook, Instagram, and TikTok to find potential fans based on their interests. Start small to test performance.
- **Optimize your profile:** Include standard info like follower counts, links to other platforms, and an email list signup link. Refresh visual aesthetics seasonally.
- **Publish regularly:** Post consistently 2-3 times per day to stay top of mind. Vary content types - photos, videos, Stories, Reels, livestreams.

Diversifying your community-building strategy creates multiple avenues for growth beyond just hoping your content goes viral. Test new tactics and double down on what performs.

Managing Online Discussions and Engagement

As communities grow into the thousands or millions, pet influencers can struggle to maintain personal engagement. Managing discussions at scale requires sturdy community management skills.

- **Segment audiences:** Consider creating exclusive groups or channels for your most devoted "VIP" fans. Host smaller Q&As just for these segments.
- **Appoint moderators:** Recruit loyal, trusted fans to help filter discussions. Give them clear guidelines.
- **Limit scope:** For unwieldy comment threads, focus on replying to just the most recent comments rather than trying to address every single one.
- **Set notifications:** Turn on post notifications for accounts you want to prioritize responding to like close friends or collaborators. Mute non-essential notifications.
- **Create FAQs:** Maintain a frequently asked questions document or video to point followers to instead of answering the same questions repeatedly.
- **Automate responses:** Use auto-reply tools to send an initial response to commenters letting them know you'll reply personally when possible.

The key is managing expectations. Transparency about your limits helps offset inability to respond 1:1 forever. Find the right balance between personalized and automated engagement.

Enhancing Community Loyalty

The most successful pet influencers don't just grow an audience – they cultivate fiercely loyal fans who rave about both the pet and owner well after the initial follow. Building true loyalty requires going above and beyond to make your biggest supporters feel appreciated.

Recognizing and Rewarding Loyal Followers

Let your longtime, highly engaged fans know how much you value them. Recognition encourages them to stick around, while rewards incentivize further participation.

- **Shoutouts:** Call out loyal fans who frequently like, comment, and share either in your content or via DMs/texts.
- **Merch:** Offer free merch like t-shirts or mugs to select superfans.
- **Real world rewards:** When appropriate, provide personalized real-world gifts like handwritten cards or care packages.
- **Virtual badges:** Create special badges, emojis, or labels for supporters who hit follower milestones or engagement thresholds.
- **Access:** Grant loyal followers access like follows back, ability to DM you, or adding to smaller private groups.
- **Collector's content:** Develop special edition content like behind-the-scenes photos only available to longtime fans.

Keep track of your most devoted followers and community members. Recognition incentivizes them to continue engaging with your pet over the long haul.

Creating Exclusive Content for Devoted Fans

Raising engagement also means crafting unique content specifically for your die-hard supporter base.

Exclusive content makes fans feel special and gives them added incentive to stick around. Ways to create VIP content include:

- **Behind-the-scenes:** Give fans peeks at candid daily life moments not suitable for your main feed. These feel more intimate.
- **Sneak peeks:** Allow devotees early access to new content before it goes out to your general audience.
- **Additional angles:** For popular main feed posts like cute pet photos, take extra shots from different angles to share just with your close supporters.
- **Making-of:** Film short videos showing how you created top-performing content, like bloopers and outtakes featuring your pet.
- **AMAs:** Host intimate ask-me-anything sessions in private groups for a smaller crowd.
- **Mobile messaging:** Use text messaging or apps to send quick exclusive photos or updates like Snapchat to loyal followers.
- **Subscriber groups:** Put superfans into smaller social media groups or channels to distribute VIP content.
- **Discussion groups:** Build online discussion forums or messaging groups to personally engage your tight-knit community.

Making supporters feel like insiders incentivizes them to keep deepening their relationship with you and your furry sidekick.

Building Personal Connections with the Audience

At the end of the day, audiences gravitate to pet influencers they feel a genuine connection with. Building authentic personal connections inspires the type of loyalty money can't buy.

Some ways to foster personal bonds include:

- **Share your story:** Open up about your own life, interests, and pets through personal vlogs, photos, and testimonials. Let your personality shine.
- **Respond to comments:** Take time to thoughtfully respond to follower comments, even just liking and reacting. This gives your community needed attention.
- **Know your followers:** Pay attention to who engages most and their personal details like pet ownership or interests. Reference and acknowledge them personally.
- **Meetups/events:** When possible based on geography and safety, arrange meet and greets with local followers. Pet-friendly events build lasting memories.
- **Send direct messages:** Proactively reach out via DM to congratulate milestones, thank superfans, and chat one-on-one.
- **Remember details:** Reference previous conversations and background details when interacting with repeat commenters. This shows you pay true attention.
- **Share contact info:** Provide followers easy contact methods like social media handles, email lists, or text community apps. Make yourself accessible.

Pet influencers who focus solely on their animals build followings. But pet influencers who share their authentic lives and personalities alongside their pets build communities. Don't underestimate the power of being real.

Final Thoughts: Building Engagement and Community

Any pet influencer can gain initial followers with adorable pet photos. But crafting long-term success means going further to actively engage audiences beyond just passive content consumption. By designing interactive content, managing communities thoughtfully, and building authentic connections with fans, pet influencers can cultivate the type of loyal, invested communities that drive real impact. Remember, your followers are not just metrics on a screen - they are living, breathing fans who want to connect. Building an ecosystem where pet devotees support and engage with each other creates a powerful force to elevate your influence to the next level. Stop thinking of them as an audience. Start empowering them as a community.

Frequently Asked Questions About Community Engagement

How can I get followers to be more engaged?

Some top ways to boost engagement include asking questions in posts, running interactive contests/giveaways, responding to comments consistently, going live, encouraging UGC through challenges, and providing behind-the-scenes exclusive content. Create interactive experiences vs just static posts.

What should I do about negative comments?

First, communicate community rules upfront that make expectations clear. Moderating and filtering when necessary is key. Respond diplomatically to negative comments that aren't abusive. Block users who repeatedly post harmful content. Disable comments as a last resort if things become unmanageable.

How often should I post to build community?

Post consistently 2-3 times per day to stay top of mind without overwhelming followers. Vary post types - photos, videos, Stories, Reels, livestreams. Monitor analytics to see when your audience is most engaged online. Posting more at those high traffic times can help growth.

How can I make fans feel more appreciated?

Loyal followers should feel valued. Provide exclusive content, give sneak peeks early access to upcoming posts, or deliver real-world gifts/rewards when appropriate. Even simple gestures like proactive DMs or commenting on their posts goes a long way. Make engagement personal.

Is it important for pet influencers to reveal personal details?

Sharing your story, interests, and life helps followers feel invested in you as a real person versus just a content source. Open up via personal vlogs, photos, testimonials or live chats. Self-disclosure breeds connection. But only share what you're comfortable with publicly.

30

Event Planning and Management for Pet Influencers

Event planning and management are crucial skills for pet influencers looking to expand their reach and engage with their audiences. Whether hosting virtual gatherings, attending industry conferences, or organizing local meetups, strategic events allow pet influencers to strengthen connections, showcase their brands, and provide value to followers. This chapter explores best practices for leveraging events to grow your pet influencer career.

Organizing Online Events

Virtual events open up new opportunities for community building beyond everyday social media interactions. With thoughtful planning and promotion, digital events can captivate existing audiences while also attracting new followers.

Planning and Hosting Virtual Gatherings

- Consider event formats that play to your strengths and interests. Popular options include Q&As, DIY workshops, book clubs, or livestreamed activities with your pet.
- Use polling features to engage attendees. Solicit questions and input to make your audience feel heard.
- Test technology and internet connections in advance. Ensure you have strong Wi-Fi and backup tech in case of glitches.
- Promote across your social channels leading up to the event. Share reminders and teasers to build anticipation.
- Offer incentives like giveaways and free digital goodies to boost sign-ups. Discount codes for your online store are another great perk.
- Record the event to share later. This expands your reach and gives attendees a chance to revisit.

Leveraging Social Media for Event Promotion

- Create eye-catching graphics and videos to promote on Instagram, TikTok, YouTube and other visual platforms.
- Go live on social media from the event itself to give followers a peek behind the scenes.
- Share behind-the-scenes photos and clips as you prepare for the event to build excitement.
- Invite co-hosts or influencer friends to help spread the word about your event.
- Monitor event hashtags before, during, and after your virtual gathering to interact with attendees.

Engaging Audiences in Digital Events

- Facilitate interactive elements like polls, Q&As, and live chats to keep attendees engaged.
- Plan special moments that spotlight your pet since followers want to see them in action.
- Review comments and questions in real-time so you can respond directly to attendees during the event.
- Share your enthusiasm and personality to create an inviting, genuine experience.
- Follow up by email afterward with a recap, additional resources, and a recording if available.

Participating in Industry Events

Industry conferences and trade shows offer unparalleled opportunities to expand your professional network and gain visibility for your pet influencer brand. With preparation and strategic relationship building, these in-person events can yield game-changing connections and collabs.

Preparing for Trade Shows and Conferences

- Research must-attend events for your niche and budget. Look for pet, social media, and influencer-focused conferences.
- Apply to host panels, give talks, or hold meet and greets if available. Position yourself as an expert.
- Create eye-catching displays, banners, business cards, swag, and promotional material.
- Set goals for new connections, potential partners, educa-

tion, media exposure, etc.
- Book accommodations and travel to maximize your time at the event. Arrive early.
- Bring along a friend or colleague for support navigating the experience.

Maximizing Networking Opportunities

- Identify key people and brands you hope to connect with. Reach out in advance if possible.
- Attend mixers, parties, and social gatherings outside main events to mingle informally.
- Introduce yourself to fellow attendees and speakers. Listen attentively and exchange contact info.
- Avoid clustering with people you already know. Step outside your comfort zone.
- Follow up with new connections right away while the event is fresh. Add on social media.
- Provide value by sharing resources and making thoughtful introductions.

Showcasing Your Pet and Brand

- Create customized branded swag like pet bandanas, toys, and treats to share.
- Bring your photogenic pet to participate if permitted and safe. Capture engaging content together on-site.
- Be prepared with elevator pitches that explain your brand and unique value proposition.
- Treat media encounters as opportunities for exposure. Offer memorable soundbites that tell your story.

- Schedule takeovers of your social accounts so your team can post live event updates.
- Express gratitude to event organizers, volunteers, sponsors, and fellow attendees.

Hosting Live Events and Meetups

Once you've built a substantial local following, hosting live meetups lets pet lovers and fans connect in real life. With thoughtful organization and safeguards in place, in-person events strengthen your community while creating memorable shared experiences.

Planning and Executing Live Events

- Scout fun pet-friendly venues like parks, stores, cafes or outdoor areas at community centers.
- Choose a family-friendly time of day and keep events 2 hours or less to accommodate attention spans.
- Handle logistics like permits, rentals, parking, bathrooms, food/water, hand sanitizer, cleanup, etc.
- Hire assistants to help with check-in, photography, activities, and pet needs.
- Collect RSVPs and have attendees sign waivers to attend. Keep groups under 25 people.
- Create a loose schedule with introductions, ice breakers, demonstrations, DIYs, and games.

Safety and Comfort for Pets and Attendees

- Set area size limits and pet ratios to prevent crowding and minimize conflicts.
- Ensure ventilation, shade, fresh water, and cleanup materials are available.
- Check with owners before interacting with pets. Respect animals' signals.
- Keep pets on leashes and separate anxious or reactive pets.
- Provide indoor relief areas in case of poor weather.
- Have emergency contact info and a first aid kit available.

Creating Memorable Experiences

- Offer fun swag bags, pet treats, and take-home activities. Raffles and giveaways also encourage engagement.
- Facilitate group photos and capture candid images throughout the event to share online.
- Build in interactive elements like Q&As, training demos, playtime, treat making, and contests.
- Insist all pet parents clean up after their animals to leave the space better than you found it.
- Follow up by email with shared photos, highlights, and feedback forms to improve future events.

Event planning requires work but yields immense rewards in terms of brand exposure, relationship building, and community engagement. With careful preparation, promotion, and execution, virtual events, industry conferences, and local meetups allow you to strengthen connections with existing followers while also introducing your influencer brand to new audiences. The chance to meet fans, collaborate with fellow creators, and showcase your pets in person creates priceless opportunities to grow your influence.

Frequently Asked Questions About Event Planning for Pet Influencers

What types of events work best for pet influencers?

Some popular event formats include virtual Q&As and workshops, industry networking mixers and conferences, pet-friendly product launches and parties, meet and greets at local pet businesses, charity fundraisers, and community pet events like adoption fairs or Halloween pet costume contests.

How can I make sure my pet is comfortable at in-person events?

Bring water, food, a crate for down time, plastic bags, favorite toys/blankets, and cleaning supplies. Monitor your pet for overstimulation. Have an exit strategy if needed. Introduce unfamiliar elements like venues in advance to get them accustomed.

What supplies should I have on hand for live meetups?

Essentials include paper goods, name tags, signage, sanitizer, cleanup bags, first aid supplies, tables/chairs, equipment for activities, promotion materials, gifts, raffle items, photography/video gear, staff, and any venue rentals required.

How far in advance should I start promoting events online?

Aim to start posting announcements and teasers about one month in advance at a minimum. Create Facebook events and pinned posts on social media to keep the details front and center leading up to the event date.

What types of items make good swag or gifts for event attendees?

Popular options include pet bandanas, toys, bowls, and treats. You can also do custom items like t-shirts, buttons, bags, and mugs with your pet's image or influencer branding. Offer discount codes for your online store merchandise as well.

31

Diversity and Inclusion in Pet Influencing

Promoting Diversity in Pet Influencing

The world of pet influencing has exploded in popularity in recent years. With so many cute and talented animal stars sharing their lives online, it's easy to get caught up in the fun animal antics. However, it's important not to lose sight of the need for diversity and inclusion within this growing community.

Representing Different Breeds and Species

While many of the most popular pet influencers are dogs, it's essential to represent the full spectrum of domesticated animals. Cat influencers have a vibrant online presence, yet other pets like rabbits, guinea pigs, and birds are underrepresented. Showcasing a wide array of species promotes inclusivity and allows niche communities to develop around less common pets.

Within dog influencing especially, certain breeds tend to dominate, like Golden Retrievers, French Bulldogs and Pomeranians. But highlighting talented dogs of all backgrounds is key. For example, Pit Bulls and other bully breeds face stigma, so influencers that showcase their sweet, funny sides provide much-needed positive representation.

Inclusive Content Strategies

Creating content that appeals to a diverse audience takes awareness and intentionality. Using inclusive language, avoiding stereotypes, and ensuring accessibility are foundational.

Subtitle and caption videos to aid hearing-impaired viewers. Describing imagery helps visually impaired fans enjoy the content. Providing image descriptions makes posts more accessible and allows screen readers to convey visual information.

Ensuring representation of diversity in videos and photos also promotes an inclusive environment. Collaborating with influencers of different backgrounds and abilities expands your reach and helps normalize diversity.

Supporting Diverse Voices in the Community

Elevating minority voices is another key strategy. From LGBTQ+ pet owners to influencers with disabilities, highlighting underrepresented groups provides role models and community for niche demographics within pet influencing.

Follow and engage with influencers outside your own

experience. Amplify posts from diverse creators. And suggest collaborations that allow unique perspectives to shine. An inclusive community requires conscious effort, but pays dividends in creativity, innovation and impact.

Inclusive Marketing and Branding

As a pet influencer collaborates with brands, maintaining an inclusive mindset in marketing and branding is essential. Avoiding cultural appropriation or insensitive portrayals allows you to appeal to a broader demographic.

Understanding Cultural Sensitivities

Cultural appropriation is an unfortunately common issue, even inadvertently. For example, dressing pets in Native American headdresses or Buddhist monk robes can be highly offensive. Research common examples of inappropriate cultural use to avoid missteps.

Understanding holidays like Cinco de Mayo, Lunar New Year and Pride Month enables you to create content that honors these celebrations authentically. Learn about the cultural significance and consult members of those communities to ensure you handle marketing and branding around these events respectfully.

Creating Content that Resonates with Diverse Audiences

When partnering with brands, look for opportunities to create content that speaks to minority groups. For example, showcasing pet products geared toward Black pet owners allows you to organically include more representation in your posts.

Depicting holidays like Diwali or Kwanzaa provides exposure for celebrations outside the Christian mainstream. Featuring influencers from diverse cultural backgrounds also widens your appeal.

Collaborating with Diverse Brands and Influencers

Seeking partnerships directly with minority-owned businesses diversifies your affiliate portfolio. Look for brands founded or led by marginalized groups. Supporting these companies expands your reach to niche cultural markets.

Collaborating on giveaways or social campaigns with influencers outside your demographic introduces your brand to new communities. A partnership between a disabled activist and a mainstream influencer raises visibility for disability issues while expanding both participants' audiences.

An inclusive business and marketing strategy allows your personal brand and content to resonate with more diverse groups. By being proactive and avoiding assumptions, you can build an authentically welcoming community.

Advocating for Inclusion and Equality

Beyond inclusive content and marketing, pet influencers have a unique opportunity to advocate for marginalized groups. Your platform amplifies messages of acceptance, empowerment and justice.

Raising Awareness on Accessibility Issues

Over 61 million adults in the US live with a disability. Ensuring accessibility in public spaces, travel and entertainment remains an ongoing need.

Influencers can raise awareness on issues like wheelchair access, sensory accommodations and access for service animals. Featuring spots that welcome those with disabilities highlights businesses doing it right. Calling out accessibility gaps encourages change.

You can also support campaigns for policy reform, like improved accommodation laws. Use your platform to educate on challenges faced by disabled citizens regarding issues like flying with service animals. Progress comes from awareness.

Championing Causes for Minority Communities

LGBTQ+ individuals still face discrimination, bullying and stigma. Transgender rights, same-sex marriage and adoption access remain contentious issues where influencer advocacy makes an impact.

Racial justice efforts also need voices on social media. Pet influencers can participate in hashtag campaigns, social media blackouts and fundraisers supporting Black Lives Matter, Indigenous rights and other anti-racist causes.

Collaborating with activists on giveaways or donation drives leverages your audience for change. Join other influencers in vocal support of equality to magnify marginalized voices.

Encouraging Diverse Participation in Pet Influencing

Finally, work to make pet influencing itself more diverse and welcoming. Encourage minority fans to start accounts for their own pets. Collaborate with new creators from underrepresented groups to widen the community.

Financially support minority influencers by purchasing products or donating to their care funds. Share their content and suggest paid partnerships to get their accounts monetized.

A conscious effort is required to build a truly inclusive field of pet influencers, but the benefits are immense. The varied perspectives and unique contributions of marginalized creators enhance the community. By embracing diversity, we move closer to the values of openness and equality that draw so many to the delightful world of pet influencing.

Frequently Asked Questions

How can pet influencers avoid cultural appropriation?

- Research cultural traditions before depicting them to understand their origins and significance. Consult members of that community. Avoid using sacred artifacts as costumes. Be thoughtful about power dynamics and voice appropriation.

What holidays present opportunities for inclusive content?

- Lunar New Year, Pride Month, Diwali, Kwanzaa, Ramadan, Hispanic Heritage Month and Native American Heritage Month allow for content that represents marginalized groups. Avoid superficial approaches and collaborate for authenticity.

Why is disability awareness valuable for pet influencers?

- With a large disabled audience, ensuring accessibility is both ethical and strategic. Raising awareness also encourages policy reform for inclusion. Featuring disability rights campaigns educates on key issues.

How can pet influencers support racial justice?

- Amplify Black voices, collaborate with BIPOC influencers, participate in hashtag campaigns, share anti-racist resources, and use your platform to promote equality and inclusion.

What steps make the influencer community more diverse?

- Encourage minority fans to create accounts showcasing their pets. Collaborate with diverse voices. Provide financial support through donations or paid promotions. Share and engage with their content.

32

Content Diversification and Innovation

In today's rapidly evolving digital landscape, simply churning out blog posts and social media updates is no longer enough to captivate audiences. To stand out, pet influencers must embrace content innovation and diversification across formats, platforms, and topics. This chapter explores strategies to create breakthrough content that wows and delights your followers.

Exploring New Content Formats

Gone are the days when a cute photo or short video sufficed on social media. As consumer expectations rise, pet influencers must get creative with content formats to foster genuine engagement. Consider these emerging content types to stay ahead of the curve:

Experimenting with Emerging Content Types

- **Interactive content:** Quizzes, polls, surveys, contests, and other interactive formats allow followers to actively participate rather than just passively consume. Tools like Typeform and SurveyMonkey facilitate creating sleek interactive content quickly.
- **Shoppable content:** Instagram and Pinterest now allow embedding shoppable tags in posts. Collaborating with brands to create shoppable pet product roundups or gift guides provides value to your audience.
- **Educational content:** From simple how-to tips to online courses, educational content establishes your authority in the pet space. Utilize multimedia formats like videos, infographics, and slide decks to teach followers new skills.
- **AR/VR content:** Immersive augmented and virtual reality content offers powerful storytelling capabilities. Though still nascent for pet influencers, AR filters and VR videos present potential for innovation.
- **Voice skills:** Develop custom Alexa skills that offer a personalized voice experience for your brand. Consider including fun games, audiobooks, or ambient sounds to delight users.

Integrating Mixed Media and Interactive Elements

Rather than just using text and photos, incorporate mixed media to boost engagement:

- **Video:** Short videos allow showcasing more of your pet's personality. Go behind-the-scenes, share day-in-the-life vlogs, create slow motion shots, and more.

- **Live video:** Live streams make followers feel part of the real-time action. Broadcast short spur-of-the-moment videos to bring authenticity.
- **Audio:** Produce a weekly podcast sharing insider stories and interviews. Audio is an intimate format that builds connections.
- **Infographics:** Combining visuals and text in infographics simplifies complex topics for pet owners. Infographics get more social shares than text-only posts.
- **Memes:** Funny, sharable memes resonate widely on social media. Use trending formats with your pet's photos or artwork.
- **GIFs:** Animated GIFs grab attention in the feed. Capture funny or cute moments with your pets and generate shareable short-form content.
- **Interactive charts/calculators:** Enable followers to personalize recommendations with custom calculators, quizzes and data visualizations. These tools boost engagement.

Pioneering Unique Content Approaches

To stand out from the pet influencer crowd, develop signature content formats:

- Spotlight rescued pets with emotive photo series and videos documenting their journeys. Tug at heartstrings to inspire adoption.
- Create a recurring advice column addressing common

questions from pet owners. Take on an authoritative tone as "Dear Abby" for animals.

- Launch a documentary series on YouTube highlighting serious issues like animal homelessness and abuse. Take an edgy, hard-hitting journalistic approach.
- Develop premium courses teaching specialized skills like training assistance dogs or mastering competitive obedience. Establish expertise with educational content.
- Curate products for monthly subscription boxes tailored to different pet types and owner needs. Offer exclusive, personalized value.
- Host a weekly podcast featuring conversations with fellow pet influencers on trends, challenges and growth. Provide an insider perspective.

The key is creating content that engages audiences in new ways. Keep pushing boundaries instead of relying on formulas.

Balancing Evergreen and Trending Content

Succeeding as a pet influencer requires blending timeless evergreen content with timely trending topics. Here's how to achieve the right balance:

Creating Timeless Content with Long-term Value

Evergreen content remains relevant regardless of when readers consume it. Focus on universal topics to extend content shelf life:

- **Pet care basics:** Housetraining, nutrition, exercise needs, grooming, health—these fundamental topics always appeal to pet owners.
- **Pet product reviews:** Share honest, in-depth reviews of your favorite toys, gear and accessories. These posts hold lasting value for buyers.
- **Pet-friendly travel tips:** Recommending pet-welcoming hotels, restaurants, parks and destinations provides evergreen assistance.
- **Training and behavior advice:** housetraining and curbing behavioral issues are ongoing needs. Address common challenges with authoritative tips.
- **Pet rescue stories:** Emotive tales of adopted pets overcoming adversity tug heartstrings timelessly.
- **Pet humor:** Funny memes, comics and lighthearted stories consistently entertain animal lovers.
- **Informational guides:** "How to" articles on topics like "How to Travel with a Dog" or "How to Correct Problem Cat Behaviors" offer enduring help.
- **Pet advice columns:** Share wisdom addressing common questions from pet owners. The issues remain relevant for a long time.

Making evergreen content is about tapping into subjects with universal, long-standing appeal to pet lovers.

Quickly Adapting to Current Trends

While timeless evergreen content forms your content base, you must also address timely trending topics to attract new audiences:

- **Holidays:** Create themed posts for holidays like July 4th, Halloween and Christmas. Include DIY decorations, gift guides, pet costumes, and celebration ideas.
- **Seasonal content:** Tailor content to seasons like providing winter care tips or sharing summer hiking trails. Align with what's top of mind currently.
- **Pop culture references:** Blend trending shows, games, songs, memes into content for fresh takes. Pop culture spices up evergreen topics.
- **Product roundups:** As new pet products, toys and gear launch, quickly curate lists and reviews while buzz is high.
- **Pet-friendly travel hotspots:** Stay on top of up-and-coming pet vacation destinations and experiences like dog cruises.
- **Current events:** Weave in mentions of cultural moments and news when relevant to your niche.
- **Viral animal stories:** Comment on and create content around viral pet stories and phenomena.

With a pulse on trends, selectively pursue timely hooks that resonate with your audience while retaining most content's evergreen nature.

Strategic Planning for Content Mix

Aim for roughly a 70/30 split between evergreen and trending content. Take a tactical approach:

- Maintain an editorial calendar mapping out evergreen content topics to cover each month. This provides consistency.

- Keep a running list of timely trending topics that arise to tap into opportunistically. These add freshness.
- Strike a middle ground in headlines. Include keywords targeting evergreen searches but add trending terms or pop culture references to stand out.
- Promote evergreen content periodically on social media to maximize its shelf life. Repurpose it into new formats like videos or podcasts.
- For extensive trending topics like holidays, create a mix of evergreen guides and highly specific seasonal posts to saturate appeal.
- Find the intersection of trends and evergreen material. For instance, tap into seasonal travel trends with pet-friendly destination guides.

With the right strategy balancing enduring and timely content, you can attract both new readers capitalizing on what's hot while also building an archive of go-to resources.

Innovating with Technology

Leveraging cutting-edge technology in content creation differentiates you while improving content quality and effectiveness. Explore these tech approaches:

Utilizing AR/VR in Content Creation

Immersive augmented and virtual reality technology presents exciting content innovation opportunities:

- Create AR pet filters akin to Snapchat and Instagram

filters followers can use on their own pets for shareable content.

- Build VR experiences putting users right alongside your pet's adventures from a first-person perspective.
- Incorporate AR features into a mobile app like 3D animations and embedded product images or videos.
- Produce 360-degree videos of pet experiences like dog park trips for immersive viewing.
- Develop AR-based educational content such as overlays showing pet anatomy, health issues, or care demonstrations.
- Provide virtual venue walkthroughs scouting pet-friendly spots followers plan to visit.
- Partner with VR gaming companies to integrate your pets into games as characters.

As AR/VR gains traction, capitalize on its unique immersive capabilities for memorable branded content. Stay on the bleeding edge.

Exploring AI-driven Content Strategies

Artificial intelligence presents new opportunities to enhance content creation:

- Use AI writing assistants to help draft, edit, and refine content. Tools like Jasper can boost writing productivity.
- Incorporate AI-generated audio narration for blog posts and videos to provide accessibility options. Descript offers quality text-to-speech.
- Harness AI chatbots to provide interactive conversational

experiences through messaging apps, your website, or smart speakers.

- Employ smart image and video categorization with AI to automatically tag and organize your media assets for easy discovery.
- Have an AI review your content and suggest additional keywords and links to improve SEO value based on competitor and trend analysis.
- Implement AI translation plugins to repurpose English content into other languages, expanding your reach globally.

AI enables creating higher volumes of content more efficiently. Selectively embrace it to enhance content operations.

Tech Tools for Enhancing Content Quality

Numerous technology tools exist to amplify content quality:

- **Grammarly:** This AI writing assistant provides advanced grammar, spelling, and style suggestions to refine prose.
- **Hemingway App:** The Hemingway Editor makes your writing bold and clear by highlighting complex sentences and passive voice.
- **Canva:** Quickly create stunning social graphics, blog images, and videos with customizable templates.
- **TubeBuddy:** This YouTube plugin helps manage your channel and optimize video titles, tags, and descriptions for discovery.
- **dagger.io:** Dagger's AI generates high-performing headlines and subject lines for your content.

- **Loom:** Record engaging explanation videos to share online or on social media.
- **Descript:** Edit audio and podcast files with AIdriven transcription and editing tools.
- **Otter.ai:** Otter automatically transcribes meetings, interviews, and audio recordings for easy notetaking.
- **Headlime:** Headlime's AI summarizes long articles into concise highlights for better reader engagement.

The common thread is utilizing technology to streamline processes, boost quality, and create compelling content efficiently.

Final Thoughts: Content Diversification is Key for Pet Influencers

Today's saturated social media landscape demands that pet influencers deliver dynamic, multidimensional content across formats and topics. Simply sharing the occasional cute photo of your pet no longer suffices. To engage and excite modern audiences, brands must embrace content experimentation and innovation.

This means not just developing proficiency across mediums like video and podcasts, but also pioneering completely new forms of content. Look for opportunities to integrate interactive elements, AR/VR technology, and artificial intelligence within your content strategy.

At the same time, achieve balance between evergreen and trending subjects. Build a strong foundation of timeless, useful content covering core pet care subjects while also tapping into current trends and pop culture moments.

Pet influencers willing to take risks and diversify their content stand the best chance of resonating widely and forming lasting connections with followers. Don't settle for mediocrity. Raise the bar with your content to drive your brand forward. The possibilities are endless when you dare to be creative.

Frequently Asked Questions

What types of content perform best for pet influencers?

It varies, but generally short-form social media content including photos, videos, and Stories tend to gain the most engagement. Also, how-to articles and trending topic listicles often attract clicks. Shoppable and interactive content are on the rise as well.

How often should pet influencers post content?

Ideally at least 1-2 times per day on your most active platform, whether Instagram, TikTok, YouTube etc. Posting consistently nurtures your audience. Mix real-time and evergreen content.

How can pet influencers come up with content ideas?

Analyze trending topics, your competitors, audience questions/requests, current events, and seasonal moments as inspiration. Curate and repurpose evergreen content. Pursue creative formats like podcasts and AR. Collaborate with brands.

What's better for SEO, evergreen or trending topics?

Focus on evergreen topics that have ongoing search volume. But also blend in trending keywords opportunistically - just don't over-optimize solely for fleeting trends. Evergreen content will accumulate organic traffic over time.

Should pet influencers worry about reading level for content?

Yes, optimizing content for easy readability allows reaching a wider audience. Aim for a school grade 8-10 reading level. Use short sentences, avoid jargon, limit complex grammar, and define specialized terms. Break up dense text with headers, lists, and quotes.

33

Public Speaking and Media Training for Pet Influencers

Gone are the days when pet influencers could rely solely on cute photos and videos to engage their audiences. To truly thrive in today's saturated social media landscape, pet influencers need polished public speaking skills and media savvy. From delivering compelling talks to handling media interviews with grace, professional communication abilities set successful pet influencers apart. This chapter explores best practices for developing public speaking skills, acing media appearances, and connecting with audiences through masterful storytelling. Whether you're looking to land speaking gigs, get booked on TV, or simply engage your followers more effectively, sharpening your communication toolkit is a must. Let's dig into the essential skills every professional pet influencer needs.

Developing Public Speaking Skills

Public speaking can feel intimidating, but it's an incredibly valuable skill for influencers to cultivate. Speaking events and conferences offer unparalleled opportunities to expand your reach, share your message, and boost credibility. Even for established pet influencers, the prospect of facing a live audience can trigger nerves. Fortunately, with the right mindset and preparation, anyone can become an engaging, compelling speaker. Let's explore some best practices.

Overcoming Stage Fright and Anxiety

If the thought of public speaking makes your palms sweat, you're not alone. Glossophobia, or the fear of public speaking, impacts around 75% of the population. For pet influencers accustomed to the buffer of a screen, being physically vulnerable on a stage can feel daunting. Here are some proven tips for managing stage fright:

- **Remember your purpose.** Ground yourself in your passion for your pet and the message you want to share. Let that sense of purpose eclipse your nerves.
- **Visualize success.** Picture yourself calmly walking on stage and delivering your talk smoothly. Mental rehearsal boosts confidence.
- **Arrive early.** Scope out the venue and get familiar with the stage itself. Feeling comfortable in the space helps minimize anxiety.
- **Warm up your voice.** Hum, sing, or do some deep breathing exercises to relax vocal cords and dissipate

361

tension.

- **Know your material.** Thorough preparation and practice are key to reducing anxiety. When you know your stuff cold, nerves have less room to creep in.
- **Focus on your audience.** Don't get trapped in your own head. Direct your attention outward and make authentic connections.

With some experience under your belt, speaking in front of groups will start to feel natural. For now, go easy on yourself and remember that a little nervousness is normal.

Techniques for Engaging Public Speaking

Now that we've covered managing stage fright, let's explore specific techniques to captivate audiences. Great public speakers understand that giving a talk is so much more than reciting words from a script. Follow these tips:

- **Establish an immediate connection.** Whether it's a funny anecdote or a surprising statistic, start strong with an attention-grabbing hook relevant to your topic.
- **Make frequent eye contact.** Scan the whole room, pausing to truly see and connect with individuals. Avoid hiding behind a lectern.
- **Use strategic pauses.** Purposeful silences build anticipation and allow the audience to absorb key points. Let some statements hang weightily.
- **Include multimedia.** Photos, videos, audio clips, polls and other multimedia elements enliven your talk. Ensure smooth technical transitions.

- **Share stories and humor.** Well-chosen stories about you and your pet humanize your talk. A touch of self-deprecating humor also helps you connect.
- **Use natural gestures.** Allow your hands to punctuate and embellish your words naturally without distracting from the message.
- **Involve the audience.** Pose questions, kick off group discussions, or facilitate quick interactive activities to get the audience engaged.
- **Close with impact.** End strong by reinforcing your core message and issuing a clear call to action. Leave the audience charged up.

With practice and experience, you'll find your own natural public speaking style. The more you present, the more comfortable you'll feel.

Crafting Compelling Speeches and Presentations

Whether you're delivering a keynote or a breakout session, strong speechwriting skills are invaluable. Follow these steps:

- **Identify your objective.** Are you aiming to entertain, inform, inspire or persuade? Define a clear purpose.
- **Know your audience.** Understand their demographics, values, knowledge level, and interests. Tailor your content accordingly.
- **Limit your key points.** Boil your talk down to two or three core takeaways you want the audience to remember. Less is more.
- **Construct an outline.** Organize your content into a

363

logical flow complete with openings and closings for each section.

- **Incorporate stories.** Prepare relevant anecdotes about your pet influencer experiences to support your points with emotional resonance.
- **Add multimedia elements.** Include attention-grabbing visuals, audio clips, polls, Q&As and demonstrations to immerse your audience.
- **Time your presentation.** Practice with a timer to ensure your content fits within the allotted timeslot.
- **Polish your delivery.** Memorize your opening and closing remarks. Rehearse until your delivery feels organic, not robotic.
- **Prepare backup content.** Have extra stories or examples on standby to adjust the length if needed.

With a compelling, tightly crafted presentation and some practice under your belt, get ready to wow your audience!

Media Training and Interviews

In addition to speaking events, media appearances provide pet influencers with powerful platforms to share their stories and perspectives. However, excelling in interviews and on camera requires specific skills. Let's explore how to make the most of media opportunities.

Preparing for Media Appearances

When approached with a media interview opportunity, preparation is key:

- **Research the outlet.** Familiarize yourself with the host's interview style and the channel's audience.
- **Clarify the format.** Will you be live in-studio or remote? Is it a quick TV spot or a deep radio discussion?
- **Define your key talking points.** Distill your message down to three concise points you want to convey.
- **Practice bridging techniques.** Prepare transitions to skillfully bridge questions back to your talking points.
- **Rehearse.** Stage mock interviews with a friend or in front of a camera so the situation feels familiar.
- **Scout filming locations.** For TV interviews taking place in your home, find a quiet spot with soft, flattering light and non-distracting backgrounds.
- **Test your tech.** Confirm all remote video and audio feeds are functioning properly beforehand. Have backups.
- **Bring marketing collateral.** Have postcards, your latest book, or other relevant materials with you to promote at the end.

With preparation and practice, you'll feel confident and ready to share your petfluencer message with poise.

Handling Interviews with Confidence

Once you're in the hot seat, follow these tips to nail any media interview:

- **Come across warm and genuine.** Avoid stiff or overly formal body language. Speak conversationally.
- **Bridge back to key messages.** No matter the question, steer your answer back to one of your talking points.
- **Keep answers concise.** For TV especially, tap brakes on wordy responses. Practice speaking in tight soundbites.
- **Allow personality to shine through.** Don't be afraid to show some of your pet's sassy sense of humor! A touch of playful banter engages audiences.
- **Correct misinformation respectfully.** If an interviewer states something inaccurate, gently pivot to providing the correct context.
- **Cite sources.** Reference reputable sources like veterinary associations to boost credibility. Avoid stating opinions as facts.
- **Avoid criticizing others.** Take the high road. You never want to come across as negative or combative.
- **Thank the host.** Express genuine appreciation for the interview opportunity. Send a thoughtful follow-up note.

Stay poised and on message, and you'll establish yourself as an influencer media outlets are eager to book again and again!

Managing Your Public Persona

As your media exposure increases, consciously shaping your public persona becomes crucial. Consider:

- **Stick to your niche.** Consistently create content focused on your area of expertise. Resist straying off brand.
- **Set boundaries.** Decide ahead of time which personal topics are off limits for interviews and conversations.
- **Monitor your online presence.** Set up alerts on your name and pet's handle to keep tabs on what interview clips and content circulates.
- **Build a media kit.** Prepare a press packet summarizing your credentials, press mentions, hi-res photos and bios. Make it easy for media outlets to access assets.
- **Draft key messaging.** Have a short description of your personal brand, topics you're passionate about, and mission statement ready to share.
- **Control your narrative.** If any interview ever misrepresents you, politely request corrections or address it on your own channels.
- **Avoid controversy.** Don't take polarizing stances on hot button issues unrelated to your niche that may alienate portions of your audience.

The media can feel like a minefield, but following best practices helps ensure interviews amplify (rather than detract from) your expert pet influencer persona.

367

Storytelling and Persuasive Communication

Beyond individual speaking engagements and interviews, masterful storytelling and communication skills empower pet influencers to connect with audiences on a deeper level across all platforms and content formats. Let's explore impactful techniques.

Crafting Stories That Resonate

Stories stick with audiences long after facts and figures fade. To maximize the power of storytelling:

- **Spotlight your pet's personality.** Help audiences get to know your pet beyond just their cute appearance. Share funny quirks and endearing mannerisms that reveal their soul.
- **Reveal your shared journey.** Open up about your experiences together over the years, especially challenges you've overcome as a team. Vulnerability builds powerful connections.
- **Talk about transformation.** Stories that show personal growth resonate widely. Share how your pet changed your life for the better.
- **Double down on the details.** Vivid, sensory-rich descriptions like sights, sounds and textures transport audiences into the story experience beside you.
- **Structure storiespurposefully.** Use narrative techniques like dramatic arc to build intrigue and interest. Aim to elicit specific emotions.
- **Weave in takeaways.** Draw out lessons learned and

how they might apply to audiences to make your stories meaningful.

Implement these storytelling best practices across videos, blog posts, podcasts and speeches to truly move hearts and minds.

Persuasive Techniques for Influence

Beyond pure entertainment, great storytelling persuades. To influence attitudes and actions:

- **Establish credibility.** Highlight your expertise and success working with pets. Audiences are more receptive to credible sources.
- **Appeal to shared values.** Understand your target audience's worldviews. Connect your ideas to values already important to them.
- **Paint a vivid outcome.** Help your audience visualize the positive impact of adopting your recommended pet care practices in crisp, concrete detail.
- **Use inclusive language.** "We" and "our" subconsciously brings audiences into your mindset, strengthening your persuasive case.
- **Encourage them to imagine.** Invite audiences to picture themselves already acting on your suggested best practices. Mental rehearsal primes them for action.
- **Leverage social proof.** When others validate your message, audiences find it more persuasive. Share testimonials from veterinarians, clients and followers.
- **Issue a call to action.** Conclude your message with a clear

369

directive for the next step you want audiences to take, like scheduling vet visits or using positive reinforcement.

Master these techniques to inspire audiences well beyond simply raising awareness.

Connecting with Audiences Emotionally

Facts and logic have their place, but appealing to emotions is often what compels audiences to care about your pet-related activism. Consider these strategies:

- **Spotlight your pet's lovability.** Share moments that highlight your pet's inherent joy, sweetness and capacity for connection. Audiences can't resist falling for them too!
- **Pull at the heartstrings.** Vulnerable stories about rescue pets or seniors needing homes urgently tap into compassion and the desire to help.
- **Validate shared experiences.** Intimately describe experiences nearly all pet owners relate to, like new puppy chaos and the relationship over the years. Foster a sense of community.
- **Use uplifting messages.** While doom-and-gloom content raises awareness initially, positive messages focused on solutions keep audiences engaged for the long haul. Provide hope.
- **Add a personal touch.** Open up about your own experiences, struggles and lessons learned along your journey. Your openness builds trust.
- **Use sensory details.** Vivid imagery that engages the

senses helps audiences imagine the feel of soft fur or the warmth of a pet's unconditional love. Make it tangible.

· **Inspire laughter.** Smartly sprinkled humor lowers defenses and helps audiences embrace your perspective wholeheartedly. Let your pet's silly side shine.

By thoughtfully engaging both minds and hearts, pet influencers can empower audiences to truly transform how they care for animals.

Final Thoughts: Mastering Communication is Key for Pet Influencers

A cute pet alone will only get you so far. To educate and inspire audiences globally, pet influencers must hone their abilities as masterful communicators across speaking engagements, media interviews and day-to-day content creation. From overcoming stage fright, to handling interviews skillfully, to crafting captivating stories, polished public speaking and communication skills separate top pet influencers from the pack. They enable you to spread your message widely with maximum impact. The minds you change and the lives you touch make all the effort worthwhile.

FAQs About Public Speaking and Media Training for Pet Influencers

What are some tips for overcoming anxiety about public speaking?

Some tips include arriving early to get comfortable with the venue, doing vocal warmups, thoroughly preparing your material, remembering your purpose, and using positive visualization. Starting with small informal talks can also help build confidence gradually.

How can I ensure my media interviews stay on message?

It's crucial to distill your talking points down to three key messages you want to convey. Then, practice seamlessly bridging interview questions back to one of those points. Maintain control of the narrative.

What makes for compelling stories as a pet influencer?

Focus on vivid details, transformative moments, your pet's personality, and your shared journey over the years. Most importantly, draw out meaningful takeaways for audiences related to pet care or your activism. Avoid superficial fluff.

What are some ways to connect with audiences emotionally as a pet influencer?

Highlight your pet's lovability, share vulnerable stories, tap into shared experiences like the pet parent journey, and use uplifting, positive messaging. Adding personal touches and humor also helps audiences relate.

How important are public speaking skills for pet influencers?

Very! Speaking events offer unparalleled opportunities to expand your reach and share your pet care philosophy. Polished public speaking skills enable you to maximize those opportunities. With preparation and practice, any pet influencer can become an engaging speaker.

34

Long-term Brand Strategy and Planning for Pet Influencers

Developing a Vision for Your Brand

Building a successful brand as a pet influencer requires having a clear vision and long-term strategy. This provides a road map to guide your content, marketing, and business decisions. With the right vision, you can create a brand that stands out, connects with your audience, and sustains itself over time.

Setting Long-term Goals and Objectives

The first step in developing your brand vision is defining your long-term **goals and objectives**. These provide direction and focus for building your brand.

Consider what you want to ultimately achieve. Do you want to build a media company around your pet? Create a line of products? Use your influence for charity work? Land partnerships with big brands?

Setting 3-5 year goals helps you work towards a larger vision. For example, your goals could include:

- Reaching 100k followers in 2 years
- Launching a pet product line in 3 years
- Starting a non-profit for rescue animals in 5 years

With clear goals, you can then break things down into smaller **objectives** and milestones to track your progress. This could involve monthly, quarterly, or annual targets for:

- Follower growth
- Content creation
- Sales revenue
- Partnerships

Revisit your goals regularly and adjust timelines as needed. But keep the bigger picture in mind to stay on track long-term.

Crafting a Sustainable Brand Strategy

The next step is developing a strategy to achieve your goals. This means defining your brand's:

- **Target audience** - Who are you creating content for? Get very specific on their demographics, interests, and values.
- **Unique value proposition** - What makes your brand stand out? Why should your audience care about you and your pet? What value do you provide them?
- **Content pillars** - What topics and content formats will you focus on? How will you help and entertain your

audience?

- **Monetization streams** - How will you generate revenue? Ads, sponsorships, products, services, etc.
- **Growth tactics** - How will you gain more followers and reach your audience? Organic and paid strategies.

Your strategy should align with your brand's strengths and purpose. It needs to provide value and fill a need for specific viewers. And it must be sustainable avoid trends or gimmicks without longevity.

Focus on consistency, high-quality content, and continually improving. This helps build trust and loyalty with your followers over the long run.

Staying True to Your Core Values

As you grow your brand, remain grounded in your core values. These define what your brand stands for.

Some examples of values for a pet influencer brand could include:

- Promoting animal welfare
- Being authentic and transparent
- Championing adoption and rescue pets
- Creating high-quality, entertaining content
- Forming genuine connections with your audience

Integrate your values into your content strategy and messaging. Let them guide your decisions - from sponsorship opportunities you accept, to how you interact with followers.

Staying true to your values cements your brand identity. It

also attracts the right audience - viewers who share your principles. This forges lasting relationships, driving consistent
engagement over time.

Adapting to Changing Market Dynamics

The social media landscape evolves rapidly. To sustain long-
term success as a pet influencer, you must stay agile and
adaptable.

Anticipating Market Trends

Keep a pulse on market trends related to your niche. Some
examples:

- New social platforms gaining traction
- Changing pet care products and services
- Hot topics among pet owners

You don't have to chase every trend. But being aware allows
you to evaluate opportunities relevant to your brand and
audience.

Conduct market research by:

- Monitoring hashtags and conversations on social media
- Using tools like Google Trends to analyze search volumes
- Reading industry news and reports
- Surveying your audience directly for feedback

Anticipating trends ahead of the curve can give your brand
a competitive edge. You can test new platforms or content

topics before they saturate the market.

Pivoting Strategies to Stay Relevant

As the market evolves, you may need to revisit your strategy. Consider if changes are needed to stay relevant.
Examples of strategic pivots:

- **Expanding to new social platforms** - Test up-and-coming apps your audience is using. But don't abandon your core platforms.
- **Shifting content focus** - Emphasize hot topics your audience cares about. But stay true to your core content pillars.
- **Adding new products or services** - Capitalize on demand for related merchandise, events, or experiences. But don't stretch yourself too thin.
- **Refining your target audience** - Expand your niche or tighten your focus as needed. But avoid drastically switching audiences.
- **Monetization model changes** - Adjust your mix of revenue streams based on viability and profitability. But maintain revenue diversity.

Pivoting strategies requires research, testing, and analysis. Move incrementally and stick to foundational brand elements that still work. Drastic pivots can alienate your established audience.

Balancing Innovation with Consistency

When adapting your brand strategy, aim for balanced evolution. Remain consistent in some areas while innovating
tactically in others.
  Maintain consistency with:

- Your core values, vision, goals
- Overall brand identity and style
- Key content pillars and topics
- Primary social platforms and channels

Innovate through:

- New content formats, series, and guest collaborations
- Emerging social platforms to test and expand reach
- Experiential events or services for superfans
- Limited-run products tied to messaging or events
- Refreshed visual branding and content style

Strategic consistency provides stability and loyalty. Tactical
innovation keeps things fresh and engaging. Finding the right
balance is key for ongoing relevance and growth.

Succession Planning and Legacy

Looking beyond day-to-day content creation, pet influencers
should consider long-term plans for their brand's future and
legacy.

379

Planning for Future Generations

If you want your brand to outlive your own pet influencer career, develop a **succession plan**.

- **Document your brand strategy & processes** - Capture your expertise so others can maintain consistency.
- **Train and mentor potential successors** - Whether family, friends or staff, teach them your approach.
- **Define transition procedures** - Create a plan for transferring creative control and assets.
- **Consider an earn-out deal** - If selling your brand, structure payments over time based on performance. This incentivizes the new owner to preserve your legacy.
- **Retain approval rights** - Negotiate the ability to review content and branding for consistency.

With proper planning, you can ensure your brand vision carries on. This allows future generations and owners to build on the strong foundation you created.

Building a Lasting Brand Legacy

Beyond business succession, focus on building a lasting **brand legacy**. Consider:

- **Your impact on followers** - The memories, emotions, and values your brand represents.
- **Recognition and reputation** - How you contributed to your niche and industry.
- **Causes and activism** - Initiatives for social good driven

by your brand.

- **Innovation and influence** - Creative content formats, campaigns or trends you spearheaded.
- **Knowledge sharing** - Resources, education and mentoring you provided.

Aim for your brand to stand for something meaningful that outlasts you. Let your legacy be defined by the positive impact and change you created.

Preparing for Transition and Change

To sustain your legacy, prepare for inevitable transitions and change.

- **Have backup succession plans** - Accommodate unexpected events or inability of successors to continue.
- **Document institutional knowledge** - Catalog your networks, processes, insights and historical records.
- **Keep contacts and licenses current** - Maintain key relationships and legal paperwork.
- **Stay flexible** - Expect your brand to evolve further under new management.

With contingency plans, your brand can live on. Future caretakers can honor your legacy while putting their own stamp through necessary evolution.

By developing a clear vision, staying adaptable, and planning for the future, pet influencers can build a brand legacy that stands the test of time. Keep your "why" at the core, stay true to your values, and maintain authenticity. With this strong foundation, your impact and influence can continue inspiring animal lovers for generations to come.

Frequently Asked Questions

What is the most important thing when building a long-term brand strategy?

Having a clear vision and purpose for your brand is the most important thing for long-term success. Determine your core values, audience niche, and competitive advantage. Build your strategy and content to stay consistently aligned with this solid foundation, rather than chasing temporary trends.

How often should I revisit my brand strategy?

Review your long-term brand strategy at least annually. Set regular checkpoints to evaluate market changes, content performance, and follower feedback. Identify what's working well and what may need adapting. Adjust smaller objectives and tactics as needed to align with your overarching vision and goals.

What are warning signs my brand is losing relevance?

Declining follower engagement, unsubscribe requests, and negative feedback are red flags. Conduct market research to understand shifts in your niche. Analyze competitors succeeding with new approaches. Falling behind industry innovations also signals losing touch. Address issues before they become severe.

Should I pass my brand down to family or sell it?

Evaluate both options. Consider your succession plan's robustness and successors' readiness. Selling provides a clear exit while rewarding your effort. But you may get less control. Passing it down may offer more consistency, if you fully prepare heirs for the responsibility. Weigh financial, legacy, and control priorities.

How can I future-proof my brand?

Build a strong culture rooted in your values. Create efficient processes to uphold standards at scale. Document institutional knowledge. Plan for technology changes. Focus on identifying and developing promising talent. Structure your company and assets to outlive any individual. Accept brand evolution while retaining your "soul".

About the Author

Justin Anderson is a former Marketing Director for Performance Food Group and a seasoned social media expert with experience spanning iconic theme parks, world-famous restaurant chains, and large retail chains. His transition from corporate social media to pet influencing began during the pandemic, leading to the remarkable growth of his pet influencer platform. With over 30k followers on Twitter, 44 million monthly impressions, and multiple Adsense-approved websites, Justin has established a significant online presence. As the face behind @chichicrewshop and the creator of sites like socialpetworker.com and chichicrewshop.com, he has leveraged his expertise to build a thriving community and brand in the pet influencer space. His work extends to an Amazon influencer shop, amazon.com/shop/chichicrew, further showcasing his diverse skills and influence.

You can connect with me on:
- ⊕ https://socialpetworker.com
- 𝕐 https://twitter.com/chichicrewshop
- 𝐟 https://facebook.com/chichicrewshop
- 𝒫 https://amazon.com/shop/chichicrew
- 𝒫 https://bestchihuahua.store
- 𝒫 https://chichicrewshop.com

Subscribe to my newsletter:

✉ https://medium.com/m/signin?actionUrl=/_/api/subscriptions/ newsletters/5d0f0fe08f24&operation=register&redirect=https:/ /medium.com/@chihuahuas&newsletterV3=39877fc04ab5& newsletterV3Id=5d0f0fe08f24&user=Justin+Anderson& userId=39877fc04ab5&source=%E2%80%94-two_column_ layout_sidebar%E2%80%94%E2%80%94%E2%80%94% E2%80%94%E2%80%94%E2%80%94%E2%80%94% E2%80%94%E2%80%94%E2%80%94%E2%80%94-subscribe_ user%E2%80%94%E2%80%94%E2%80%94%E2%80% 94%E2%80%94-

www.ingramcontent.com/pod-product-compliance
Lightning Source LLC
Chambersburg PA
CBHW071200290526
45796CB00008B/90